STRATEGIES
FOR
SURVIVAL

PRINCIPLES OF
JEWISH COMMUNITY
RELATIONS

D1289502

STRATEGIES
FOR
SURVIVAL

PRINCIPLES OF
JEWISH COMMUNITY
RELATIONS

Walter A. Lurie

KTAV PUBLISHING HOUSE INC. • NEW YORK

Library of Congress Cataloging in Publication Data

Lurie, Walter A. (Walter Albert), 1912-
  Strategies for survival.

  Bibliography: p.
  Includes index.
  1. Jews—United States—Politics and government.
2. Antisemitism—United States. 3. Intercultural education—United States. 4. United States—Ethnic
relations. I. Title.
E184.J5L87   1982   305.8'924'073   82-18684
ISBN 0-87068-453-1

Manufactured in the United States of America

In memory of
MICHAEL RUBINOW LURIE

Contents

ACKNOWLEDGMENTS

A grant from the National Jewish Community Relations Advisory Council underwrote the publication of this book.

Albert D. Chernin, Executive Vice-Chairman of the NJCRAC, and Albert Vorspan, Vice-President of the Union of American Hebrew Congregations, read the manuscript in draft. I appreciate their interest and valuable suggestions. Jill Vincent Caslin typed the manuscript.

I thank all who assisted in this endeavor.

I am grateful to my wife, Dr. Olga Rubinow Lurie, for her discerning comments and for her constant encouragement.

I alone am responsible for the contents of this book.

W.A.L.

INTRODUCTION

Do Jews need a community relations program in the United States today? If so, what kind of program?

There is no unanimity in Jewish response to these questions. Unanimity is neither possible nor necessary. There is widespread consensus on the importance of the questions themselves for Jewish survival and creativity.

In the past, two sizeable groupings of Jews would perhaps have replied in the negative to the first question, as to whether any sort of community relations activity is needed.

The most traditional have regarded community relations efforts as a frivolous distraction from proper Jewish concerns, perhaps even as a profanation of the Covenant and a lack of trust in Divine Providence. People in this segment of the Jewish community believed that Jews can be tainted by participating in the secular culture of America. They wished to preserve the Jewish heritage by insulating themselves as much as possible from the general society, engaging in its business to live, but otherwise maintaining enclaves walled off from contamination.

Those least identified with Jewish concerns have regarded community relations programs on behalf of Jews as ill-guided assertions of Jewish distinctiveness. They believed that Jews should be perceived to differ from other Americans, if at all, only by their adherence to the "Mosaic persuasion." They would have advised Jews not to endanger their security by visibility and to mingle unobtrusively in the general culture—advice that they would give as well to Adventists, Mormons, Roman Catholics, and Hare Krishnas.

It is not my purpose to evaluate different concepts of Jewish life, but rather to point out their community relations implications. Today, the overwhelming majority of Jews in the United States are neither separatists nor assimilationists. They accept, as most Jews have had to accept through millennia, that contacts with non-Jews are inherent in daily patterns of living. Efforts to maintain benign community relationships are therefore an aspect of daily life, a matter of common sense like seeking shelter from the cold winds. Most Jews believe that a community relations program is needed.

The second question—What kind of program?—evokes a great variety of responses. Recently I overheard an argument about some of the issues.

"It's a whole new world," proclaimed Weiss. "We Jews in the United States are secure ourselves. We have to be on guard only against threats to Israel and to Jewish communities overseas. We should be having a demonstration every week. For our community relations, all we have to do is stand up proudly as Jews and speak our minds on Jewish issues."

"Weiss, you're crazy!" said Schwartz. "Anti-Semitism is alive and thriving in the United States. Why, the neo-Nazis have a bookstore two blocks from where I live, and now they want a license to parade, just like Skokie. A KKK leader was interviewed respectfully on our local television station. Christian missionaries posing as Jews have a house next to the State College campus and the Jewish kids are going in for that and for all kinds of weird cults. Minority groups we helped for years are blaming *us* for discriminating against *them*. Our local school board is planning to open the day with prayers in every class. Our Board of Elections scheduled a primary on Yom Kippur. We have to plan our community relations in recognition that it's the same as it has always been."

"You're not keeping your eye on the ball, Schwartz," replied Weiss. "Why, even the deicide charge against the Jews has been disavowed. We should concentrate on protesting anti-Zionist slander by the Arabs and the Soviets at the United Nations and on rallies for Soviet Jews. Old-fashioned anti-Semitism doesn't amount to anything. And there's no reason for Jews to worry about everyone else's civil rights and economic opportunity—those aren't Jewish community relations questions."

"You're so advanced, Weiss, that you've lost touch with reality," Schwartz rejoined. "If our small Jewish community doesn't keep working in cooperation with Christian religious, black, labor, and other groups to eliminate unequal opportunity and reduce friction, we won't be able to do anything for Israel or Jews in the Soviet Union, and ultimately we'll be isolated and defenseless."

Weiss and Schwartz were plainly talking past each other. Each is partly right and partly wrong. There are many more dimensions of controversy than could be shown in a brief example: how advisable are militant protests? quiet negotiations? subtle propaganda? pressures for legislation? explanations? litigation? etc., etc.

Jews have wrestled with such questions for centuries. Why then is there still controversy over principles instead of agreement? No two countries, no two periods are identical. Every situation is different, every case involves new questions not automatically resolved by past experience and deliberation. Besides, Jews are known for holding a diversity of opinions, and what seems right to Weiss may always be rejected by Schwartz, even when they agree on the facts. The pressures of life have necessitated rather severely focused ad hoc deliberations: What do we do now?

Scattered through the record, nevertheless, are many general principles, stated or implied. Their value has often been questioned, because their application in concrete situations is unclear. The difficulty is pinpointed in the classic story about the grasshopper who sought advice from the ant one autumn. "I've been having a great time all summer," he said, "but it's getting cold and I have no food. What can I do?" The ant thought a moment and then said, "I have an idea for you. Cockroaches live in houses, where it's warm and there's plenty to eat. Turn yourself into a cockroach." The grasshopper said, "That's a great idea! But how do I turn myself into a cockroach?" The ant said impatiently: "I've given you the principle. You work out the details."

The value of principles may nevertheless have been underestimated. Jewish community relations is an art or skill rather than an exact science. The most experienced practitioners are able to assess new situations without having to reinvent the wheel every time. Principles represent efforts to articulate this know-how. They supply a perspective distilled from much cogitation by many people under diverse circumstances. Principles are concise bits of wisdom that can initiate the young and inexperienced into the arcane processes of analysis and action.

The purpose of this book is to bring together, in a systematic framework, principles regarding community relations developed over the past forty years. They reflect the extensive interconsultation of many of the keenest minds in the American Jewish community, lay leaders and professionals, as they have grappled with concrete challenges to Jewish life and creativity.

The body of this book consists of three major sections:

Policies, the basic approaches of the American Jewish community relations program
Strategic Principles, more specific substantive guidelines for choosing tactics in a variety of areas
Procedural Principles, techniques of community relations practice, less substantive but no less important.

These principles require further analysis, situation by situation, and without specific study they cannot be applied as a guide to Jewish community relations practice. The principles were developed in the context of Jewish community relations in the United States, and are adapted to that framework. Some concepts may be applicable in other settings, but the assumption of applicability must be tested by reason and experience in the appropriate situations. One of the concluding sections of the book considers the questions of broader applicability.

Sources

Do these principles actually represent positions taken by Jewish community leaders over the years, or are they expressions of my personal opinions? Both. Let me explain.

Think in terms of *three* books of "Principles of Jewish Community Relations."

The first is *THE BOOK*. This is the totality of ongoing decisions, statements, thoughts, and actions over the years in the cause of Jewish community relations. Devoted efforts through a number of organizations, much inspiration, and the wisdom of many people have formed it. While the source of the content of this document, it is not available for study and use in any systematic way. *THE BOOK* is not all formulated in words and written down, not assembled, not classified and organized, not edited, full of contradictions that have not been confronted and addressed. It has not been updated and reviewed in the perspective of changing circumstances.

Second is *The Book,* which is the much narrower but still extensive body of statements at the level of principle that have been formulated over the years by the agencies in the field. *The Book* is of course a distillation from *THE BOOK,* and it is in writing, but it is still far from readily available for study and use. It is dispersed; bits of it were assembled at different times for different purposes and in different styles; much is extant only in dusty dead files. It has not recently been reviewed, edited, and updated.

The third is *this book.* It is what I have drawn from these sources, not a transcription of them. I have selected, organized, combined, and rewritten in order to produce a document readily available for study and use. No two people attempting such a task would arrive at identical outcomes. Therefore, while it is the aim of *this book* to convey accurately the essence of *The Book* and *THE BOOK*, I alone am responsible for its contents.

Notes indicate the sources of the policy statements and principles. Sometimes the derivations are diffuse, and the reference often takes the form, not of a quotation, but "Cf. [document and page]."

By far the most frequent sources are documents of the National Jewish Community Relations Advisory Council, the unique coordinating agency. There are two major reasons. First, since NJCRAC documents are the products of inter-consultations involving all the agencies in the Jewish community relations field, they incorporate all currents of thinking. Second, because of the nature of the NJCRAC's responsibilities, particularly in reassessment of strategies and joint program planning, NJCRAC documents contain a number of statements at the level of principle, which are less commonly encountered elsewhere.

So many good minds have participated in the framing of the basic concepts of Jewish community relations that any effort to designate special contributions may be unfair. Not all the leaders have left their marks in written materials. It would be a disservice to future generations of Jewish community relations leaders to omit altogether names of creative predecessors. With apologies to my friends (or, even more ruefully, to their memories) who made exceptional contributions but are not listed, I here acknowledge the debt of the Jewish community relations field for their part in developing its fundamental concepts to:

> First of all, my dear colleagues in the early days of the NJCRAC (then National Community Relations Advisory Council): Isaiah M. Minkoff, whose imprint on the field is beyond recounting; Arnold Aronson; Jules Cohen; Samuel Spiegler; and Albert Vorspan.
>
> Then, creative lay leaders who have contributed ably to the thinking of the field: Jordan Band, Mortimer Brenner, Julian Freeman, Aaron Goldman, Milton Goldstein, Sidney Hollander, Irving Kane, Jacqueline K. Levine, Shad Polier, Lou H. Silberman, Bernard H. Trager, Jerry Wagner, and Lewis H. Weinstein.
>
> Next, professional colleagues from national and local community relations agencies in earlier years: Harry I. Barron, Isidor

Chein, Albert D. Chernin, Oscar Cohen, Maurice Eisendrath, Benjamin R. Epstein, Maurice B. Fagan, Morris Fine, S. Andhil Fineberg, Samuel H. Flowerman, Arnold Forster, Isaac M. Franck, Lillian Friedberg, Philip Jacobson, Will Maslow, Emanuel Muravchik, Alexander Pekelis, David Petegorsky, Leo Pfeffer, Earl Raab, Robert Ephraim Segal, John Slawson, Sidney Z. Vincent, Seymour Weisman, and Ann G. Wolfe. (Subsequently Chernin and Jacobson became associated with the NJCRAC directly.)

Finally, people of vision and force who made an impact on the thinking of the field without direct association: Philip Bernstein, Dan Dodson, S. P. Goldberg, Arnold Gurin, Harry L. Lurie, Robert M. MacIver, Bayard Rustin, and Roy Wilkins.

As I put a period to the preceding sentence, a flood of other names fills my mind. I am truly sorry that this is not a full history of the Jewish community relations field in which I could recognize many other contributions.

Definitions

Certain key terms recur frequently in the following pages. For the present purposes, they can be defined as follows:

Jewish community: The assumption of this book is that a Jewish community does exist in the United States, on the basis of recognized mutual concerns. However widely they may differ among themselves—in synagogue affiliation, economic status, educational and cultural level, and social and political viewpoints—Jews in America form a community because they share

- a sense of affinity with other Jews, in this country and throughout the world
- identification with the Jewish past
- concern for the security and welfare of Israel
- concern for the Jews of the Soviet Union and other lands where Jews are oppressed and persecuted
- determination to combat anti-Semitism and all other forms of bigotry
- a commitment to democracy, justice, freedom, and equal rights in a free America
- aspirations for status for Jews as individuals and as a group, and for a favorable popular image of Jews
- a desire for positive and mutually accepting relationships with other groups in our society.[1]*

The *organized Jewish community* consists of those Jews who identify themselves actively with Jewish concerns through organizational membership or participation in community actions or services to meet Jewish needs. The *structure of the organized Jewish community* is the aggregate of organizations and agencies through which such identification is expressed. A *local Jewish community* is the organized community of Jews residing in a defined metropolitan or other cohesive geographical area, usually delimited by inclusion in a single federation and in the catchment boundaries of federation-sponsored service agencies.

Jewish community relations programs consist of those activities which are directed toward enhancement of social conditions conducive to secure and creative Jewish living. The Jewish community relations program serves the needs of the Jewish community by seeking

- to oppose anti-Semitism, bigotry, hatred, and violence
- to promote in the United States equality of opportunity, without regard to race, religion, ancestry, or sex
- to secure freedom of thought, opinion, and association
- to ensure freedom of religion and separation of church and state

*See Notes and References, pp. 132 ff.

- to encourage amicable relationships among all groups
- to interpret Israel's position and needs to the American public and government
- to marshal public opinion in behalf of justice and freedom for Soviet Jews and other oppressed Jewish communities.[2]

A *Jewish community relations agency* is a continuing body, usually with volunteer board and professional and auxiliary staff, and financed principally by federation or other organized Jewish community contributions and/or membership dues as a Jewish organization, which in furtherance of the Jewish community relations program as described above conducts all or some of the following kinds of activities:

- campaigns of public education and interpretation, through newspapers, magazines, radio and television, publications, speakers' platforms, and all other media
- continual contacts with legislators and public officials
- public statements, congressional testimony, and other formal presentations
- court actions or *amicus* briefs in suits instituted by others
- cultivation of working relationships with non-Jewish or cross-sectional groups—religious, labor, professional, educational, ethnic, women's and veterans' organizations, and others
- public meetings, rallies, marches, picketing, demonstrations to focus public attention on issues and causes.[3]

There are also ad hoc agencies, e.g., the National Conference on Soviet Jewry.

In general, Jewish community relations agencies are non-political, not-for-profit organizations which are tax-exempt and tax-deductible under Section 501 (c) 3 of the Internal Revenue Code.

A *national Jewish community relations agency* is one with a constituency drawn from a number of areas in various parts of the nation, maintaining a program and resources designed chiefly to deal with matters that are national in scope. A *local* Jewish community relations agency's program and resources are, on the other hand, addressed chiefly to the concerns of Jewish groups in the area served. A local Jewish community relations agency (usually called Jewish Community Relations Council or JCRC) is said to be *representative* if it has the participation of all the significant organizations and groups in the community. National agencies in general are not designed to be representative in this sense; rather, each serves as the nationwide expression of its constituents, cutting across geographical areas. The constituents have been drawn together by some specific approach or ideology or other link as the basis for affiliation. Membership is selective rather than cross-sectional.

There is also one national *agency for cooperation and coordination* in the Jewish community relations field, the National Jewish Community Relations Advisory Council (NJCRAC). Its members are eleven national agencies* and over one hundred local Jewish community relations agencies. NJCRAC is not a separate functional community relations agency, but a process through which the autonomous national and local member agencies seek voluntary agreement.[4] Local cooperation and coordination are responsibilities of the JCRCs, which also have functional responsibilities in their areas.

A *Jewish community relations leader* is a man or woman, volunteer or professional, who has been elected or appointed to a board, officership, committee, or staff position in a national or local Jewish community relations agency that involves prominent and active participation in the formulation and implementation of policy and programs.

A *professional Jewish community relations worker* is a paid male or female employee of a Jewish community relations agency who bears responsibility at a level requiring judgment, initiative, and skill for the implementation of Jewish community relations program.[5]

The *Jewish community relations field* is the aggregate of

*American Jewish Committee, American Jewish Congress, B'nai B'rith–Anti-Defamation League, Hadassah, Jewish Labor Committee, Jewish War Veterans of the U.S.A., National Council of American Jewish Women, Union of American Hebrew Congregations, Union of Orthodox Jewish Congregations of America, United Synagogue of America/Women's League for Conservative Judaism, and Women's American ORT.

organizations, agencies, resources, leadership, and personnel entrusted by the organized Jewish community with direct responsibility for Jewish community relations programs. This is a collective term, and does not necessarily imply unanimity or lack of dissent within the field.

POLICIES

The Jewish community relations program has undergone extensive evolutionary development in the past forty years, reflecting changes in the world and in the situation of American Jewry. This period witnessed Hitler's ascendancy and defeat, and the continuing turbulence in social and international relationships in the postwar world. The purpose of the following paragraphs is to highlight some of the major changes in concepts as they have grown out of changing conditions.

Development of the Jewish Community Relations Field

The contemporary pattern of Jewish community relations work is an American invention, but it was not created out of thin air. It is the inheritor of a long tradition that embraced intercession by court Jews (*stadlonim*), formation of officially recognized Jewish communities or *kehillot,* social action and community representation by rabbis and congregational leaders. The Jewish community adapted to its own purposes the typical American social agency structure of volunteers and staff. In the early years of this century, the national, and later the local, community relations agencies were established, with involvement of diverse elements in the Jewish community.

The national agencies originated as the independent expressions of the interests and wishes of separate internally like-minded constituencies. They differed in ideology, concerns, and even to some extent in place of family origin and role in American Jewish life. B'nai B'rith, the oldest Jewish service organization, was established in 1843. In the course of time, it sponsored health, cultural, geriatric, and a variety of other Jewish agencies, including the Anti-Defamation League in 1913. The ADL was founded to protect the good name of the Jew and to combat all intergroup stereotyping. Congregational bodies in the three principal Jewish

denominations, appearing after the middle of the nine-
teenth century, addressed themselves to issues of religious
freedom. The American Jewish Committee was established
in 1906, following the Kishinev pogroms, to urge appropriate action by the United States against such outrages. The
Jewish War Veterans of the U.S.A., going back to post–Civil
War days, has always defended Jewish rights. The American
Jewish Congress in 1922 grew out of an effort following
World War I to make sure that the needs of the shattered
Jewish communities of Europe were given adequate attention in the peace-treaty-making process. The implementation of the Balfour Declaration was also a major concern.
The Jewish Labor Committee, an expression of the secular-
ist, Yiddishist, trade-union-oriented segments of the Jewish
community, became active in 1934 to combat the growth of
Hitler's power. Hadassah, a Zionist organization, the National Council of Jewish Women, a service group interested
in immigration and in children's needs, and the Women's
American ORT, a vocational training and rehabilitation
agency, grew into community relations programming as
necessary extensions of their original programs for Jews.
Local agencies came into being in the larger cities in the late
1930s and early 1940s, when Hitler agents and home-grown
Hitler imitations were trying to poison the minds of the
American people.

In their early years, these agencies were small and com-
manded no great resources. Each agency was busily engaged
in reacting as its constituency saw fit to situations they
deemed threatening to Jewish security, and indeed in the
1930s the field was called "Jewish defense" or, more ele-
gantly, "civic protective work."

The rise of Hitlerism in Europe and the threat of the anti-
Semitic German-American Bund and Silver Shirts in this
country stimulated growth and concentration of activities.
Others besides Jews were aware of these menaces, thus
giving Jewish community relations agencies further access to
the larger American scene. Increased activity by each agency
multiplied the possibilities of duplication and crossed wires.
This simultaneously stimulated cooperation among the

agencies themselves and the demand within the broader Jewish community for much more coordination.

Local agencies were established in the larger centers of Jewish population, as more and more Jewish organizations in each city became involved in dealing with the problems. These JCRCs supplied a democratic forum for the expression of diverse views. The movement to create local Jewish community relations agencies quickly spread from the largest cities to every sizable Jewish community, bringing into the process the federations, which until then had concentrated on philanthropic services for Jews.

A coordinating instrumentality for four large national agencies, the General Jewish Council, was unable to surmount the differences among its members. In 1944 the General Assembly of the Council of Jewish Federations established the National Jewish Community Relations Advisory Council (NJCRAC, then just NCRAC), the first fully viable process for cooperation in the Jewish community relations field, since it involved both national and local agencies.

The name of the coordinating agency contained the new term "community relations," which quickly supplanted "Jewish defense" and "civic protective" as the designation of the field. This change in terminology signalized a highly meaningful development in the concepts and practices of the agencies. Narrowly defensive reactions to threats initiated by anti-Semites were transformed into the current processes of positive programming and the planning of self-initiated forward actions on the broad social scene. However long-range, of course, programs had to be constantly adapted to specific needs and circumstances.

Since the life-or-death struggle against Nazism, the United States has emerged as the dominant power in the free world, and national allegiances have become polarized between the United States and the Soviet Union. Other momentous events and social changes have included the creation of the State of Israel; the "Black Years" under Stalin, the Night of the Murdered Poets and the Doctors' Plot, followed in the 1970s by the incredible emergence of the Jewish movement in the U.S.S.R.; the Six-Day War and the Yom Kippur War; Vatican II and the Roman Catholic Church's abrogation of the charge of deicide; notable Supreme Court decisions on church-state issues and the school desegregation decision in 1954; the Civil Rights Act of 1964; the burning of the cities in the 1960s (and bit by bit ever since); alienation and disaffection among young people, fluctuating in intensity but always present; OPEC; the drive for women's equality and the resistance to it; the Soviet- and Arab-sponsored Big Lie in the United Nations that Zionism is racism; the Camp David agreements and the peace treaty between Israel and Egypt; and, most recently, far-reaching changes in American public opinion and electoral preferences, leading to shifts in economic and social policies.

Some of these developments are clearly negative. Others are positive, and some represent the fruition of years of planning and effort, in which Jewish community relations agencies played active, and not infrequently leading, roles. The more destructive situations have had to be parried, to minimize harmful effects. There has been no scarcity of items on the American Jewish community relations agenda. The following *broad policies* have guided the Jewish community relations field over these years.

1. The General Welfare

The Jewish community relations field seeks to advance the general welfare and to strengthen American democracy, regarding these as the basic guarantees of Jewish security.[6]

Discussion: What this means is that Jewish community relations work goes beyond concrete problems whose Jewish relevance is immediately perceptible. In the broader context, whatever contributes to the general welfare strengthens democracy and therefore is valuable to the Jewish community. Obviously some limits to agency programs are necessary because the Jewish community's resources are not boundless. It is necessary to set priorities in order to mount an effective program. But the simple test "Is it good for the Jews?" is met by any action for the general welfare.

This very broad principle is the absolute foundation of all

Jewish community relations work in contemporary America, and as a policy it is universally accepted by community relations leaders. Who would defend the proposition that Jews would be more secure in a less democratic nation? That Jews could enhance their well-being at the expense of, rather than in harmony with, the general welfare?

For years, the annual Joint Program Plans of the NJCRAC have contained the statement that the "social conditions conducive to secure and creative Jewish living . . . can be achieved only with a societal framework committed to the principles of [democracy and equal rights, spelled out in detail]. History has bred in Jews the deep conviction that such social conditions, which accord with ethical and religious values derived from Judaism and Jewish tradition, afford Jews, and all others, the best opportunity to enjoy secure and meaningful lives."[7]

But Jews would not be Jews—in fact, would not be human—if there were no differences in the interpretation and application of so broad a policy. What are the threats to American democracy today? How can the general welfare be defined, when many groups in America have conflicting specific objectives?

Of course such questions can never be resolved unanimously or finally. For more specific guidance, the current consensus can be consulted in each year's NJCRAC Joint Program Plan, which offers analysis and recommendations. The 1981–82 JPP devotes many pages to issues covered by this policy, taking positions on economic and civil rights questions very closely aligned with those of previous years.[8] The recommendations are cautiously stated, of course, because there is less than complete agreement on specifics; but the basic necessity of programming in the areas of the general welfare is strongly reaffirmed.

2. Democratic Pluralism

The Jewish community relations field fosters democratic pluralism, believing that the source of the greatness of the United States and its hospitality to Jews is its success in bringing together people of many origins, religions and groups on the basis of equality.[9]

Discussion: The principle of democratic pluralism, while no more self-interpreting than the policy of advancing the general welfare, is also universally accepted by Jewish community relations leaders. Both elements in this policy are essential: pluralism and democracy.

The more nearly homogeneous a society is in any respect, such as ethnic composition (e.g., Japan or Sweden) or religious affiliation, the less likely is full acceptance and opportunity for a group differing from the overwhelming majority. If times are good and the cultural tradition includes hospitality to strangers, a prosperous life may be possible for limited numbers of individuals from other groups, on the basis of tolerance rather than true acceptance. The "guest" individuals usually do not assert group identity, either because of insufficient strength or to avoid being looked upon as freakish. Assimilation and ultimate disappearance by absorption or emigration threaten tiny minorities in homogeneous societies. If economic conditions should become poor, or if the dominant culture is distrustful of outsiders, newcomers must keep their bags packed and regard themselves as temporary sojourners. Happily for Jewish community relations, the United States is not a homogeneous society.

It can be maintained, of course, that no large industrial nation today is homogeneous. Gilbert and Sullivan may be right that an Englishman remains an Englishman, but a Cornishman is a Cornishman and most definitely not a Yorkshireman, and a Kentishman is not a man of Kent, who lives on the other side of the little river Medway. Regional, economic, occupational, educational differences exist in every large country. There are no closed countries today, and the whole world is moving toward pluralism. The point is not whether conditions are terrible for Jews in more homogeneous societies elsewhere, but that American pluralism is good for Jewish community relations.

In this country there are few families who have to go back more than two generations to find roots in one of a number of foreign cultures. There are many American church bodies each of which has more than a million adherents. A person with a foreign accent, even one who does not speak English, is not a curiosity. Blue eyes and brown eyes, curly and straight hair, and, yes, dark and light skins and round and slant eyes are widely accepted as part of the American mosaic. Whatever tendency there may once have been for *Mayflower* descendants or First Families of Virginia to try to define and uphold an American norm has long since disappeared in American pluralism.

The other equally essential element is democracy. Not every mixed country is democratically pluralistic. The old Austro-Hungarian Empire contained dozens of ethnic groups, as does the Soviet Union today. The boundaries-by-fiat of many postcolonial nations, particularly in Africa, embrace peoples differing in ethnicity, language, and religion. Latin American countries have absorbed varieties of immigrants, but with strong pressures to assimilate to the life patterns set by the dominant class.

In most of these situations there is no pretense of democratic pluralism, but only overt dominance by the group that can get on top, sometimes with continuing conflict and upheavals. In the Soviet Union, division into ostensibly autonomous regions is substituted for genuine pluralism. This led to the absurdity of trying to herd the Jews to remote Birobidjan.

The United States is democratically pluralistic, one of a very few nations which are both pluralistic and democratic, such as Canada and Israel. It is essential for Jewish welfare that the American Jewish community relations program foster democratic pluralism.

3. Majority and Minority

The Jewish community relations field does not recognize any group in this country as a majority, entitled to set the norm of Americanism, nor does it regard the Jews (or any other group) as a minority which is part of the American scene only on sufferance and at the price of conformity.[10]

Discussion: At one time some members of the Jewish community were seeking "tolerance" as a goal of community relations efforts. It is now recognized that being tolerated means acceptance of second-class citizenship, and therefore is a denial of equality.

This policy is an extension of the universally accepted principle of democratic pluralism. However, it has unfortunately been muddled by semantic confusion.

Simple arithmetic establishes that some groups are more numerous than others. Perhaps this finding is not so simple. Population statistics is an inherently tricky field of study, as the troubles of the U.S. Census Bureau attest. In any case, religion is not analyzed in census figures. Still, it is obvious that there are more adherents to the Roman Catholic religion than to Judaism in the United States, more people with light skins than with dark skins, more people with round eyes than with epicanthic folds, more who speak English in the home than speak Spanish. Technically, therefore, there are of course larger and smaller groups, and some aggregates may add up to more than 50 percent, which is the dictionary distinction between "majority" and "minority."

Even statistically, however, it can be shown that there is no meaningful majority group in this country—only a mosaic of minorities.

What are some of the candidates for majority status? Is there a Christian majority? Only in the crudest sense. Roman Catholics, Southern Baptists, Armenian Orthodox, and African Methodist Episcopalians are all Christian denominations, but there is not much evidence that they form a cohesive group. Is there a white majority? What is a white? Are Hispanics white? Are only descendants of Europeans and Mediterranean peoples white—that is, Swedes in Minnesota, Poles in Chicago, Sicilians in New Jersey, Jews in Los Angeles, Basques in Nevada, Lebanese on Atlantic Avenue in Brooklyn, English in Appalachia? Is there now a native-born majority—native-born descendants of immigrants, that is, not Native Americans, the American Indians—as compared with the foreign-born? Of course there is, but the strength of ethnic identity shown in the Northern Ireland and Polish and Israeli crises and the lapel buttons saying "Kiss me, I'm Italian" show that the native-born have not been homogenized.

There is a further and different semantic confusion reflecting the complexities—and realities—of intergroup relations in the United States today. The well-intended regulations designed to benefit people who have suffered from past discrimination, economically and in terms of status, are probably necessary. They designate the proposed beneficiaries as "minority groups." People who need and want these special provisions are therefore happy to proclaim themselves "minorities," and jealously defend their right to the designation. Blacks and Hispanics are "minorities." Each of these is a much more numerous group than the Jews, who are not an official minority. People of Asian and Native American descent are "minorities," and sometimes, by a peculiar twist of logic, so is that majority of the population which is female. The term "minority" is used as a circumlocution for "disadvantaged" or some other opprobrious designation. My point is not that the actions are right or wrong, but that this is a special usage of the word "minority."

In asserting the policy that no group in this country should be regarded as a majority or as a minority, I am using terminology that might be rejected by the official "minority groups" who wish to continue to receive the benefits provided for them by law. But their leadership would agree with Jewish community leaders on the policy itself, that no group can or should proclaim itself the right-thinking majority pace-setters, with all others relegated to the status of also-rans.

Related to the problem about the designation "minority" is another semantic confusion, fortunately no longer sanctified by law in this country, but historically even more significant, involving the word "race." Respectable anthropologists once used the term in an effort, never very successful, to categorize populations by physical and presumably genetic characteristics and to trace the migrations and origins of ancient peoples. The term was utterly debased by Hitler and his pseudo-scientific "scholars," through glorification of the "Aryan race" as superior and calumniation of all "non-Aryan races," specifically Jews and blacks, but also many others. Neither Aryans nor Jews form a "race" in any sense used by reputable anthropologists.

It is a destructive term. If mankind were divided into races, and these races were genetically different, then surely it might be possible that some races could be superior to others, the inferior races. Jews had hoped that this myth of racial superiority would be permanently effaced from serious discourse after the almost mortal struggle of the free world against Hitler's vicious doctrines. But in recent years the blacks, perhaps as an act of defiance against know-nothing backwoods prejudices, and the Hispanics, who were comparatively untouched by the Hitler madness, have each independently begun to use the term "race" in a positive sense as the badge of their proper feelings of group identity. Such primitive survivals as Afrikaner *apartheid* have helped keep the concept alive. In this country, "racism" is the most widely employed designation for harmful actions on the basis of anti-black prejudice. Around the world, the word "racism" is used pejoratively, and very loosely, by Soviet propaganda to slander Israel, the United States, and other free-world nations. Formerly colonial nations, including at least one in which black slavery is still practiced, join in condemning democratic Israel as "racist."

The implications of the word "race," certainly since Hitler, are that birth is destiny and intergroup relations can never be posited on the assumption of human equality. These meanings are surely not intended by any group in America today, except for a tiny remnant of unregenerate red-necks and a few disturbed Nazi imitators. Jews can only deplore the use of this destructive term—now so widespread that it is difficult to avoid resorting to it—and regret its injection into the legitimate process of upholding group identity. Like the term "minority group," "race" confuses the issues of democratic pluralism. But if blacks or Hispanics want to apply it to themselves in a positive sense, so be it.

4. Group Identity and Expression

The Jewish community, like other groups in this country, maintains its own cultural and religious distinctiveness while participating fully through group and individual expression in general American life and affairs.[11]

Discussion: As part of the American mosaic, Jews as Jews have the right to speak out on public issues—such as policy toward Israel, the implications of the federal government's budget, and school decentralization. This is an obligation of good citizenship. Not only do Jews have the right, but they can expect questions to be raised by others: What is the Jewish position on South African *apartheid?* on Northern Ireland? etc. Of course, no one can speak for "the Jews," only for organized Jewish structures. And since resources are limited, it is not necessary that a position be expressed on every issue of the day—a concentration on those most clearly germane to current concerns is understandable. But it is no longer acceptable to limit Jewish participation in current issues to the separate actions of individual Jewish citizens. Group expression and action are implied in American democratic pluralism.

At the time of the French Revolution, liberal leaders were eager to advance the emancipation of the Jews, just then emerging from medieval restrictions. The slogan was: "To the individual Jew, everything; to the Jews as a people, nothing." This was perhaps a reaction against the artificial community structures imposed on the Jews (and other distinctive groups) by various despotisms as the instruments for externally enforced discipline, but it represented nonetheless a homogenizing tendency.

In the early years of the present century, the Jews who had arrived long before and were well established felt threatened by the strangeness of the Jewish greenhorns just off the boats. They founded settlement houses to "Americanize" the newcomers, fearing that their own security and prosperity would be diminished if the general American public took alarm at the flood of unacculturated Jews. These attitudes persisted in one form or another until recent years, giving rise to anxiety on the part of some established Jews about any conspicuous display of action, opinion, or conduct of Jews as Jews—even the reading of a Yiddish newspaper in the subway. Democratic pluralism was not yet fully accepted in American society generally, and there was some basis in reality for these concerns. As recently as the early 1950s, Professor Robert M. MacIver, in a study commissioned by the Jewish community relations agencies, gave less than a full endorsement of the policy of group identity and expression.[12]

The concerns of the Jewish community leaders about democratic pluralism have been considerably mitigated since then. Not only Jews but many other groups were represented in large numbers among the immigrants to the United States. Each resisted complete acculturation and clung to its own distinctiveness in many respects. Perhaps most important of all factors, American-born children of the immigrant groups began to establish themselves as well-to-do, well-educated, and politically potent elements on the American scene, without experiencing any need to distance themselves from their several group identities.

But the policy of group identity and expression still raises questions in application. One reason may be that some Jews have interpreted it as a mandate for public expression by Jews as Jews on every issue. Statements have been made in the name of the Jewish community when in fact Jewish opinion was divided or unformed. Public statements have frequently been made with no thought or provision for follow-up, as though statements alone constituted program. This is, of course, the negation of planning. Also, public statements have been made, contrary to another basic policy, without regard to the frequent need for enlisting the participation of other groups.

One leading community relations theoretician has distinguished between "instrumental" techniques, designed to achieve an outcome, and "expressive" techniques, effective merely in relieving feelings.[13]

Thus the application of the policy of group identity and expression, a valid derivative of the principle of democratic pluralism, always requires careful consideration and planning. The policy, of course, applies only to issues, not to political campaigns and elections. At the polls, Jews and members of all other groups in the American mosaic vote their individual consciences and judgments.

5. The American Creed

The Jewish community relations field honors and relies upon the American Creed, the ideal of equal rights derived from the Bible, as embodied in the Declaration of Independence and institutionalized in the Constitution and Bill of

Rights and in the laws and regulations of the federal government and the several states.[14]

Discussion: This policy means that the survival and well-being
of every group that has suffered discrimination and prejudice rest upon the democratic ideals and institutions of this
country. Extremists of the right and left may challenge the
American Creed, either to substitute other ideas (e.g., the
natural superiority of some group) or to assert that a fundamental change (e.g., a revolution) would bring equal rights
more effectively than the American system; but the Jewish
community relations field rejects these fringe views.

The American Creed has been the subject of much cynical
scoffing, as a pie-in-the-sky dream far from reality. But many
polls and long-range analyses of public opinion continue to
show that, despite vicissitudes, the great majority of the
people think of themselves as well-meaning and the United
States as a just society.

Of course it would be a mistake and a deception to set
forth a Pollyanna or a Dr. Pangloss principle. The United
States is not paradise, and not everything that happens
always happens for the best. The question is not whether our
country is perfect, but rather, what is the best policy for
attempting to remedy its imperfections. It is precisely because of the American democratic process that remedies are
possible.

Popular and community support have been mobilized for
community relations goals by showing that they are derived
from American ideals. When first proposed, measures for
fair employment practices or school desegregation or fair
housing, for instance, were attacked as radical or alien ideas.
The advocacy has rested on the convincing demonstration
that they implement basic American ideals. Educational and
interpretive programs are more readily understood and
accepted if their message is, "This will realize the American
dream," whereas they are more likely to be rejected if they
say, "Everybody else has been wrong—now listen to this!"

The alternatives to citing the American creed are not
promising ways of achieving community relations goals.
Would the Jewish community's aims be advanced by attack-

ing American ideas, laws, and institutions? By saying, or even implying, that the United States has failed from the beginning and should start over again? That they do things better in Sweden or Canada or Israel or France or the Soviet Union?

At the time of this writing there is a serious danger to the American Creed because of an insidious movement for a Constitutional convention. This has gained support because the American people as a whole have not recognized it as a threat to the Bill of Rights. It is being promoted quietly in state legislatures by those who oppose equality and recognition of the rights of all. The urgency of this problem shows the importance, however Panglossian it may sound, of clinging to and defending the American Creed.

6. The American Way

The Jewish community relations field advances the national interest of the United States when it seeks to eliminate imperfections in the implementation of the American Creed.[15]

Discussion: This is the complement of the policy of relying on the American Creed. It means that the implementation of the American Creed is good for America, and that America suffers to the extent that there are gaps and resistances in implementing the ideal of equal rights.

A distressing number of social problems today reflect the discrepancy between American ideals and their realization in actuality. Crime in the streets, family disorganization, underachievement in school, vandalism, voter apathy, are only a few of the symptoms. These indicate the alienation from other segments of our society of those who are so disadvantaged that they have given up any expectation of equal treatment.

The United States has become great because it has been able to evoke and hold the loyalty and affection of the many groups making up its population. The American Creed has made this possible; some have been able to realize the promise, and others, still striving, have found a source of hope. Lapses from basic American ideals have cost the country dear and have had to be corrected: the evil stain of black slavery, the exploitation of *braceros,* the Japanese detention camps of World War II. Adherence to American ideals has made the Statue of Liberty's torch a symbol of U.S. leadership for people's rights, throughout the world. Mistakes and departures from the ideals have created much frustration and confusion, in this country and abroad.

Short-sighted special interests from time to time defend practices or propose measures in basic conflict with the American Creed of equality—sometimes disguising their meaning with misleading patriotic slogans. Community relations programs opposed to these errors are not endangering this country's welfare through softheartedness. They hold the high ground of hard-nosed patriotism, and challenge the lapses in the name of the American way.

7. Interdependence

When one group in American society, such as the Jews, acts to uphold the American Creed, it advances the interests of all groups in the country whose rights have been impaired or endangered.[16]

Discussion: This principle recognizes that all groups in American society have a common interest in correcting imperfections in the realization of the American Creed. Therefore, there is a basis for joint action.

Because of differences in situation among groups, this principle may be difficult to apply in practice. The leadership of one group or another may differ with most Jewish leaders about the way, in fact, to support the American Creed. For instance, among recent conflicts with groups that have often engaged in joint action with the Jewish community are differences with Roman Catholics on the support of nonpublic schools, with blacks on quotas, with labor unions on immigration policy, with liberal Protestants on policy in the Middle East, with political leaders on the relative primacy of tax cuts or human services, and so forth.

But these tactical differences do not negate the principle. In fact, a reshuffling of the issues shows simultaneous common action with the same groups in other contexts: with blacks and liberals on voting rights, with trade unions on social reform, with Roman Catholics on undocumented aliens, and so forth. Policies necessarily transcend tactical specifics.

8. Coalition

For the Jewish community, or any other group, to pursue its interests effectively in the public arena, common effort with others is essential.[17]

Discussion: In this large and varied country, public opinion is responsive to many different influences, and public officials have to reconcile the demands of many groups. Even a large group, forced to go it alone, may find that its strength is not sufficient to achieve its objective.

The Equal Rights Amendment has not been passed, although women are more numerous than men. There are many reasons for this, and women have not been united on the issue. While ERA is designed to guarantee equality for men and women alike, not every pro-ERA campaign has stressed common-interest aspects of the issue.

Blacks have bitterly opposed the elimination of Great Society benefits, which are also needed by members of many other groups, but the articulate black campaign for a number of reasons has not gained much support. Because this is seen by some as just a black issue, the campaign has not as yet shown progress.

The Jewish lobby is allegedly strong, but both the Reagan and the Carter administrations were able to defeat it on the arms-to-Saudi-Arabia issue, in part because this was successfully misrepresented as merely a Jewish issue and failed to attract many previous coalition partners.

The coalition policy also requires that each group seeking to align joint efforts for a goal of particular interest to itself must, from time to time, endorse some of the cherished goals of those whom it desires as partners. While the principle of interdependence establishes that there is a basis for joint action in the need to correct imperfections in the realization of the American Creed, compromises at the tactical level are necessary to win support. These need not involve yielding on fundamentals.

Even when controversies have become bitter, as with the blacks on quotas, the Roman Catholics on parochial-school appeals for public funds, the Protestant liberals on the Palestinian Arabs, both sides recognize the need for common action on those objectives that are shared. Thus each group is required to reach for and emphasize the universal elements in its particular concerns. There are obviously differences in each group's specific goals, but the solid basis for common action is some genuine element of shared interest, even if no more than exchange of support for each other's priorities.

STRATEGIC
PRINCIPLES

Broad policies and principles establish a general framework within which more specific strategic and tactical decisions must be made. Yes, the Jewish community relations program is designed to advance the general welfare; yes, it fosters democratic pluralism; yes, it relies on the American Creed and aims to remove imperfections blocking equal rights; yes, it seeks these goals through a coalition policy based on common interest. But how is all this to be done?

The strategies, techniques, and tactics of Jewish community relations have been so diverse over the years, and so closely adapted to changing situations, that it would be impossible to attempt an exhaustive summary. Analysis and interpretation; statements, public events, and rallies; intergroup and interreligious cooperation; attention to newspapers, films, radio and television, and other media; formal educational procedures and contacts with schools and colleges; maintaining relationships with public officials and other influential persons; legislative research, litigation, and contacts with public administrative bodies—these are only a few of the program instrumentalities that have been and still are in use, with a great variety of approaches. Each can be valuable if well and skillfully used; each can be wasteful or even disastrous if applied dogmatically by formula and without the necessary continuous study, thought, and cooperation in use of resources.

The answer to the "How?" question is always specific. It requires a detailed ad hoc analysis of the problem and situation, possible courses of action and their advantages and disadvantages, and the alignment of forces.

The gap between the general policies and the specific tactical decisions can be bridged somewhat by strategic principles. These are closer to the situational actualities but still broad enough to cover a range of approaches. They define a less extensive area within which answers to current problems can be sought without canvassing all possibilities afresh.

Strategic principles derived from experience over many years are discussed below under the following headings:

Jewish Security in a Free Society
Social and Economic Justice
Religious Freedom and Church-State Relationships
Interreligious and Intergroup Relationships
Education and the Schools
The Mass Media of Communication
American Jewry, World Jewry, and Geopolitics

The following strategic principles are for the most part derived from the ongoing processes of planning and evaluation within the National Jewish Community Relations Advisory Council. Some have been formulated in the analyses required for the annual Joint Program Plans, which are adopted formally each year by representatives of all the Jewish community relations agencies. Organizational dissents are noted.

Many of these principles were developed in a series of reassessment conferences. These have brought together community leaders and subject-matter experts, Jews and non-Jews, for three-day focused discussions, on the basis of extensive background materials, concise presentations, and hours of face-to-face discussion in small working groups.[18] They have included:

Community Relations Values of Interreligious Activities, 1953

Overt Forms of Anti-Semitism, 1953

Advancement of Community Relations Objectives by Law and Legislation, 1954

Use of the Mass Media of Communication for Community Relations Purposes, 1956

Community Relations Work with Children and Youth, 1957

Respective Roles and Responsibilities of Private and Public Agencies in Advancing Community Relations Objectives, 1958

Strategies and Approaches in Implementing Policies on Religion and the Public School, 1961

Community Relations Components in the Work of Other Jewish Communal Services, 1962

Combating Anti-Semitism Today, 1968

The Public Schools and American Democratic Pluralism— The Role of the Jewish Community, 1971

The Mass Media, the Image of Israel, and U.S. Foreign Policy, 1980

Reassessment reports are issued in the names of those participants who endorse them. Dissents are noted.

Jewish Security in a Free Society

A principal task of the Jewish community relations field is that of maintaining the security of the community. At the time of the Hitler threat, protection against anti-Semitism was a major preoccupation; in times of less-visible menace, it remains an essential responsibility that cannot be neglected.

In order to cope effectively with problems of security, the Jewish community relations program must address such questions as these: What is the current status of Jewish security? What are the trends? What is the nature of existing and potential threats to Jewish security? Under what conditions might security deteriorate? How can anti-Semitism be combated? The following strategic principles deal with these and related questions.

9. Status of Anti-Semitism

Despite fluctuations in overt anti-Semitic manifestations from year to year, the Jewish community relations field does not regard the present level of anti-Semitism in the United States as a serious threat at this time.[19]

Discussion: This is a basic judgment for programming. It is, of course, situationally conditioned, and it could change with time and circumstances. It is not merely a finding of fact— seriousness is not a fact, but a judgment. Such indications as assaults on Jews and Jewish institutions, the extent of discrimination and prejudice against Jews, and the acceptance of anti-Semitic personalities and organizations are significant criteria. By any measurement, these have declined rather than increased over the last forty years. The principle is based on the assumption that it is not necessary to take emergency steps regarding anti-Semitism as though there were a serious menace to Jewish security at this time.

In 1968 the reassessment conference on anti-Semitism made an optimistic assessment of the Jewish position in the United States.[20] It pointed out that Jewish group status was high in America, that Jews were upwardly mobile economically and socially, that the group status of Jews is equated with that of Catholics and Protestants, that Jews, regarded a generation ago as poor immigrants, are now seen as members of an influential, well-educated, affluent group, the very embodiment of "the establishment."

Since then there have been flare-ups of KKK activity, public disturbances by neo-Nazis, and sporadic synagogue and cemetery vandalism, but on a very small scale and never with any indications of public support for the anti-Semites. In Argentina, in France, in Austria, and of course always in the Soviet Union, there have been some extremely disturbing organized anti-Semitic actions and expressions, and virulent anti-Semitism can spread to our shores if it is not stopped. The king of Saudi Arabia has honored special guests by giving them beautifully bound copies of that noxious forgery, *The Protocols of the Elders of Zion*. But after weighing these and other developments, the most recent judgment, in the 1981–82 Joint Program Plan, is: "On balance, we believe that Jews are secure in America."[21]

The Jewish community relations program must cope with anti-Semitic manifestations, and the following principles deal with some approaches; but this strategic principle means that, as of now, it would be a mistake to push the panic button.

10. Latent Anti-Semitism

The Jewish community relations field regards subsurface anti-Semitism as persistent and potentially threatening.[22]

Discussion: Anti-Semitism is unique in that, unlike other group prejudices, it is deeply embedded in Western culture and religion. Certain Christian teachings, and specifically the deicide allegation, have long been recognized as major sources of anti-Jewish feeling. These are acquired so early that they become part of the body of unexamined convictions many people take for granted. People believe these doctrines without bringing them to awareness, where they might be challenged by fact and observation.

In recent years Christian leaders, in this country and around the world, have made efforts to combat anti-Semitism. The Vatican under Pope John XXIII led other churches in an effort to counteract the charge of deicide and to correct the presentation of other church teachings that might perpetuate anti-Semitism. Yet studies show that eradication of these prejudices is a slow business. The interpretations of Christian doctrine that gave rise to much anti-Semitism continue to have significant effects.

There are other anti-Semitic myths and stereotypes not of an obviously religious origin, such as the ascription of hateful racial, economic, and personal characteristics to "the Jews." These continue to circulate at a low level of visibility, mostly in the poorer and less-educated segments of the population. They surface quickly in moments of stress or anger—a fight with a landlord, a complaint about a business deal, a neighborhood quarrel, a political campaign. Adolescents, looking for a little excitement, manage to stir some up when they daub a swastika on a synagogue or gravestone or on a neighbor's door.

These low-key or episodic reminders of virulent anti-Semitism may have little significance in themselves and generally can be dealt with calmly and soon disappear. But they serve as important reminders that while overt anti-Semitism has been out of fashion for many years since Hitler gave it a bad name, the substratum still exists. A spark can start a conflagration.

11. Danger Signals

While combating such overt forms of anti-Semitism as violence, vandalism, and defamation, the Jewish community relations field maintains a constant watch for potentially dangerous organized and political forms of anti-Semitism.[23]

Discussion: Spontaneous overt expressions of anti-Semitism are always dismaying. Two other elements which must be present for latent anti-Semitism to grow to Hitlerian dimensions, however, are not in evidence today. These are the growth to substantial dimensions of an organization dedicated to the spread of anti-Jewish propaganda and action, and the systematic use of anti-Semitic scapegoating in the political arena, either by a charismatic bigot or by coldly calculating power-brokers. These would be significant danger signals.

There are a few dedicated anti-Semitic groups still in existence or becoming visible from time to time. The Ku Klux Klan has some persistence, and there are small pockets of neo-Nazis here and there. They are internally divided, because of the incompatible personal ambitions of the would-be Hitlers who recruit small followings. They scatter their fire, not sure whether it is the Jews or the blacks or the trade unions or the liberals that they want to deal with first. Most of them have little money, and they have not succeeded in penetrating respectable power centers. They do not loom as prominent forces in public opinion. Indeed, when non-Jews think of them at all, most seem to regard them as ridiculous crackpots rather than as imposing forces.

On the political scene, no openly bigoted figures have had any success. The very few candidates in various 1980 local elections who featured anti-Semitic scapegoating were overwhelmingly defeated by constituencies in which Jews were only a very small fraction. Jews have been elected in largely non-Jewish districts.

While the Jewish community must ever be sensitive to warning signals and to possible serious developments, it is also important not to tilt at windmills. Polls consistently show that Jews fear anti-Semitism disproportionately to the salience of anti-Jewish attitudes, which in fact play a very minor role in general public opinion. Jewish overanxiety can lead to unnecessary and unwise measures. There are genuine intergroup differences in the political arena, as on quotas or tax credits for non-public-school education. As with other political struggles, rhetoric can be bitter on issues of this sort. When there have been public expressions by Jewish groups on such issues, there may be harsh criticism, not only of the positions taken, but of the organizations and Jewish persons who have spoken out. Public debate must not be confused with anti-Semitic libels, canards, or unjust stereotyping.[24] Of course when anti-Semitism lurks beneath the mask of legitimate discussion of issues, it must be exposed and attacked. Delicate analysis of specifics is essential.

Purposive organization and political exploitation of anti-Semitism are very serious danger signals. Today these seem most frequently to involve anti-Israel and anti-Zionist propaganda, which are discussed in a later section. The question for consideration now is: Under what conditions can a serious threat to Jewish security arise?

12. A Menace to Jewish Security

Even without explicit anti-Semitism, the Jewish community relations field recognizes a deep menace to Jewish security arising from malfunctions and crises in our society that could threaten American democratic life.[25]

Discussion: The danger to Jewish security is not limited to overt and explicit anti-Semitism. There may be anti-Semitic consequences without specifically anti-Semitic genesis. Jewish landlords are attacked when there is a rent squeeze, Jewish stores are looted when there are riots, Jewish intellectuals are harassed when there is a mass panic about avant-garde ideas.

Lying close to the surface, and breaking out from time to time, is a pervasive climate of anxiety, distrust, and frustration. Unemployment, decaying cities, rising crime, rebelling youth, changing moral codes have spread disillusionment and discontent. The foundations of social order and mutual confidence have to some extent been undermined, and terrorism, violence, and confrontation have appeared in struggles over issues in this country as well as abroad. Violent actions have evoked the reciprocal use of force to counter them, fanning hostility and heightening tension.

There is thus an ever-present threat, fluctuating with changing circumstances, to the stability of the American socio-political system. This danger comes not only from the extremists who may instigate disorders, but also, and possibly more seriously, from those who would in reaction impose "law and order" through a regime of police repression. Rigid and extreme expressions of opposing views can lead to polarization and harsh confrontations. History shows that Jews are always among the first to suffer under such circumstances. If there should be a pernicious deterioration of the quality of life and political process in this country, the same consequences could result here.

13. Civil Liberties

The Jewish community relations field regards the rights of freedom of expression, association, and assembly as essential to the security of Jews, as of all Americans, and therefore seeks to protect the civil liberties of all.[26]

Discussion: This strategic principle is clearly implied in the preceding statements, but there has been controversy within the Jewish community regarding its application in a number of situations. Recent examples have been the extensive and protracted conflicts over the march in Skokie of a band of neo-Nazis, and the debates over the syndication of a television interview in Philadelphia of a KKK leader.

The question, essentially, is whether the civil libertarian slogan of "Freedom for the thought you hate!" may not be quixotic in some circumstances, and dangerous for the Jews and for democracy. One contention is that Nazi propaganda is not free speech, but the perversion of free speech, aiming to abolish all freedoms; that it is insidious, contagious, and inherently destructive; and that it therefore has no right to be admitted to the free marketplace of ideas.

The counterarguments are various: that no legal ways can be devised to bar anti-Semitic propaganda that would not also impair unobjectionable utterances found offensive by one crank or another, thus ultimately stifling Jewish expression as well; that disproportionate efforts to stop crackpots from making fools of themselves in public may result in larger and more sympathetic audiences for their venom than they might otherwise have had; and that existing laws against fraud, libel, and incitement to riot offer sufficient protection against extremists. To start a conflagration, it is noted, both dry tinder and a spark are needed, and the sparks will do little damage as long as the tinder is wet (i.e., as long as the conditions for potential social instability are not at flash point).

It is difficult to draw the line between prior suppression and censorship, on the one hand, and legitimate protest, on the other. Painstaking analysis is required to distinguish between wise reliance on American democratic institutions to survive petty hatemongers, and pusillanimous failure to halt inciters of bigotry who cross the boundaries of legitimacy. But the principle of civil liberties is valid. Jews are necessarily nonconformists in our society. Jews need the protection of the Bill of Rights, and must preserve it. This is not a self-destruct plan; it places no obligation on the Jewish community to facilitate or accept hostile expressions or actions. Since there are nonsectarian resources for defending civil liberties, which have by and large received the endorsement and support of Jewish organizations, the Jewish community relations agencies at times may find greater priorities for their limited resources than civil liberties issues. This is always an ad hoc decision.

The NJCRAC Joint Program Plan for 1981-82 strongly reaffirms the importance today of the principle of civil liberties: "The Bill of Rights is the bedrock of American freedoms. The governing principles . . . are our national articles of faith. . . . Whoever seeks to set them aside strikes at the very heart of the Bill of Rights, the American Creed."[27]

14. Combating Anti-Semitism

Since anti-Semitic acts and expressions are widely recognized to be dangers to all Americans rather than to Jews alone, the Jewish community relations field seeks and expects the cooperation of general community resources in combating anti-Semitism.[28]

Discussion: The many forms of anti-Semitism, actual and potential, require different forms of treatment. They all rest on the assumption that anti-Semitism is rejected by the overwhelming majority of the American people and by the officials whom they have elected to positions of authority, an assumption borne out by experience and by polls and studies over the years. Specific measures, of course, depend upon analysis of the situation, and can be widely varied. Some of the techniques and approaches that have been used include the following:

a. *Exposure and condemnation* (i.e., making known to a wide public the facts about an offending person or organization) have gained in effectiveness when appropriate, as anti-Semitism has come to be regarded as disreputable in itself. Because an accusation of anti-Semitism can be very damaging, Jewish agencies make such accusations only on the basis of solid and incontestable evidence. The decision was sometimes made deliberately to take no action on specific anti-Semitic episodes and utterances, but American news media have made deliberate inaction no longer effectual. It is not possible to smother the facts of bigotry.

b. *Quarantine,* an alternative to public condemnation, involves persuading the media that a given anti-Semite and his utterances and activities are not worthy of the publicity that he so avidly seeks. Quarantine differs from merely ignoring the offender. Judgments of the applicability of this approach require taking into consideration the prominence of the anti-Semite and the extent of his access to public attention. It is manifestly not applicable to public officials, legislators, or others whose views automatically receive publicity because of their status. Quarantine is different from censorship, which is rejected because it is violative of civil liberties.

c. *Legal action and police activity:* Laws on the books protect against many forms of discrimination. Police activity is of great importance in connection with violence and vandalism. Since these are sensitive issues, the Jewish community relations agencies recognize the need for special orientation and training for the police in understanding problems of intergroup tension. Many of the offenders are young people who have not settled into fixed patterns of hostility against Jews, and counseling by a clergyman, teacher, or social worker may be advisable. In general, the law should be enforced as it would be if no anti-Semitism were involved; seeking severe punishment to make an example of the offender may be unjust and unwise, whereas an unduly light sentence might erroneously suggest community approval of the offender's conduct. Arresting anti-Semitic defamers is not feasible or productive, since courts uphold the constitutional freedom of speech, even bigoted speech.

d. *Education,* by means of interpretation in both popular and scholarly media of the socially destructive nature of anti-Semitism, is a basic and essential aspect of the Jewish community relations program. Urging tolerance and recounting Jewish contributions, once widely used, are now recognized to be demeaning, ineffectual, and irrelevant.

15. Cults and Conversionary Movements

The Jewish community relations field resists and regards as harmful the denigration of Judaism and Jewishness by cults and conversionary movements.[29]

Discussion: One particularly persistent insult to Jews and burden on relations between Jews and non-Jews over the centuries of Diaspora has been the constant pressure for conversion to the dominant religion of the nations in which the Jews have lived. In pluralistic America, where freedom of religion is guaranteed in the Bill of Rights, conversionary pressure has taken different forms. In some ways, the situation has become more confusing than in countries with a single dominant religion, as many different groups have sought conversion of Jews to their diverse faiths. A common aspect of conversionary efforts, all through history, has been the denigration of Jewish religion and life.

While no Inquisition need be feared in this country, on the American scale there seems to have been some worsening of the situation in recent years. The general malaise and alienation which set in at the time of the Vietnam War have stimulated a countertendency toward seeking security in absolute faith and fanatical conviction. Those who feel that they have achieved undeniable revelations wish to pass them on to others; those who are still struggling with the ambiguities of life are easily tempted to try one certainty or another.

Some conversionary efforts are conducted by Christian evangelists of unquestioned sincerity pursuing what they regard as their religious mission. Others with more dubious credentials advance spurious arguments that Judaism is compatible with acceptance of Jesus as divine. There is also a variety of exotic cults and movements whose recruitment methods exploit sophisticated techniques of psychological suasion and whose rituals seem calculated to induce surrender of intellectual autonomy by the converts. How large the inroads have been is a matter of speculation.

At meetings conducted by conversionary groups, Jewish community relations agencies can and should challenge publicly statements that misrepresent Judaism and denigrate Jewishness. Since such groups sometimes use false and misleading names in announcing their events, Jewish community relations agencies should expose any deceit and misrepresentation to public notice and to appropriate authorities. This will not damage, but will have a positive impact on, interreligious relationships with the conventional Christian religious groups, most of which are willing to join in public denunciations of the cults, their methods, and the harmful effects on the individuals snared by them, which may include some of the children of their own congregants.

Jewish community relations agencies, of course, recognize the primacy of constitutional guarantees of religious freedom, and do not condone harassment of cults in the absence of unlawful actions. But claims to constitutional rights do not absolve acts in violation of law; criminal acts should be prosecuted as the law provides. Since the most fanatical and extreme movements are clearly outside the bounds of general community acceptance, the Jewish community can confidently expect intergroup endorsement of its planned and rational efforts to protect itself, in accordance with this strategic principle.

16. Rejection of Violence
The Jewish community relations field deplores, condemns, and rejects all extralegal forms of violence by or on behalf of Jews against anti-Semites or presumed enemies of Jews.[30]

Discussion: This principle is accepted as basic by all the major Jewish organizations in this country. It is challenged by small segments of the American Jewish community, such as the Jewish Defense League. These challengers regard themselves as the only steadfast and courageous defenders of the Jewish people against anti-Semitism, neo-Nazis, and the KKK, and the only determined proponents of Jews in the Soviet Union and in lands of oppression.

The rejection of violence rests directly on acceptance of the principle of the American Creed. It is specific to this country, where the laws and basic institutions are friendly to Jews, as to other religious and ethnic groups in the American mosaic. Of course the principle is not meant to rule out the use of appropriate force by constituted legal authorities when necessary in carrying out their responsibilities to protect Jews and other citizens, nor legitimate measures of self-defense.

Direct action or militancy by Jews may be required at times, such as in the form of civil disobedience or resistance to unfair local prohibition of a peaceful demonstration. Illegal violence, however, is counterproductive. It seldom succeeds in eliminating, or even frightening, the presumed enemy. In fact, the victims of such harm as may be inflicted are usually innocent bystanders, as in the bombing of a Nigerian diplomatic-license car in front of the Soviet mission to the United Nations. Violence alienates public opinion—if anything, it arouses sympathy for its targets. Of more direct importance, it also alienates supporters among officials, police, and influential leaders.

The perpetrators of counterviolence have fallen into a trap. In advocating this method of protecting Jewish security, they actually undermine it. They contribute to a vicious cycle of mounting violence that may ultimately cause polarization and weaken American democracy. This is obviously self-defeating.

17. Program for Jewish Security

The fundamental strategy of the Jewish community relations field to preserve Jewish security is that of alliance with the self-corrective forces in American society, for the elimination of injustice and poverty, and for the protection of freedom, constitutional rights, and democratic processes.[31]

Discussion: The specific techniques for dealing with anti-Semitic manifestations do not constitute a complete program for Jewish security. It is necessary in today's world for Jews, as individuals functioning within nonsectarian movements and organizations and through Jewish community organizations, to deal with the large-scale issues that affect the welfare of our society, on the merits of the measures for preserving and advancing a democratic pluralistic society.

Programming must maintain a community atmosphere in which the cooperation of the general community is always available. The general community resources are brought to bear on both the long-range and immediate problems of anti-Semitism by developing and fostering mutual respect and cooperation among all groups every day in the year, rather than by neglect of daily relationships and frantic appeals for help when an emergency arises.

Social and Economic Justice

The biblical injunction to pursue justice has always guided the Jewish community. The moral obligation has been strongly reinforced by the practical realization that Jews are part of the general American society, prospering as it gains and certain to be affected negatively in bad times.

Comparatively few in the present generation of Jews have encountered barriers to their own access to the good things of American life. The imperative of equal justice for all may therefore seem impersonal to them, a matter of pure altruism. The perspective of time shows that this is an unwarrantedly optimistic judgment.

The father of a young Jewish graduate from an Ivy League college quite possibly was rejected by the same institution, not on grounds of merit, but because of a discriminatory quota, a *numerus clausus*. There were many firms and industries and occupations closed to Jews. In actuality, the successful young Jewish executive or professional can recognize that, consciously or automatically, *he* had to sidestep many still-existing barriers and choose a field in which a Jew can advance (and *she* may have had additional problems as a woman, but that is another part of the story). Restrictive housing covenants have been eliminated, but Jews tend to cluster in sections where they know they are not unwelcome.

The same is true of clubs and recreational facilities and resorts.

Against blacks, Hispanics, Orientals, and the poor generally, discrimination is still clearly evident. The most complete holdover from the evil days of black slavery—segregation— has been mitigated but far from eliminated. The goal of integration is seldom challenged frontally, but every practical means to advance it—busing, affirmative action, open housing—arouses controversy and resistance. Even the equal protection of the laws is questionable in many sections of the country.

The dubious status of civil rights is not the only imperfection in this country's realization of the American Creed. In a land of vast resources, natural and human, there is poverty, and even hunger. Amidst a people with countless unsatisfied needs, there are millions of workers unemployed and underemployed.

America's problems are far from universal or overwhelming, and in comparison with most other countries the United States measures up well. Yet every person who suffers needlessly is a challenge and a rebuke to those in a position to help. Furthermore, history shows that the persistence of such social ills poisons relationships within a society and can ultimately undermine even the strongest institutions.

The following strategic principles address the role of the Jewish community in relation to social and economic justice in American life. They have been developed from experience over a number of years and under changing economic and social conditions. As principles, they are broad and general in nature, bridging the wide range of views within the Jewish community and transcending shifts in national public opinion about approaches to the general welfare. Controversies may have developed in the application of the principles, and these will be discussed in relation to each of the strategic guidelines.

18. Unfinished Tasks

The Jewish community relations field recognizes the continuing imperfections in American life as threats to the social stability of our democratic nation.[32]

Discussion: The imperfections of democracy are at all times a very serious affair. In periods of social stress and crisis they become the weak links in our social structure against which attacks on democracy can be launched. In too many areas of our social life, democracy is incomplete because such factors as color or creed or origin are used to deny people their legitimate rights.

It is therefore necessary, where democracy is incomplete, to extend it and safeguard it. Wherever the democratic rights of any group are curtailed, there is a threat to the security of all.

The consequences of the denial of rights go beyond the deprivations of the individuals suffering discrimination. When people are crowded into inner-city slums, the results are tension, crime, and sickness. When justice is not equal, when the poor are disproportionately given long terms in unlivable prisons, Attica-style rebellions result to shake our whole society. When full access to higher education or professional training is denied, the entire country is deprived of a source of talent and skill.

19. Political, Economic, and Social Democracy

The Jewish community relations field regards political, economic, and social justice as interdependent and inseparable aspects of American freedom.[33]

Discussion: This strategic principle follows from the broad policies and the specific considerations of the nature of Jewish security in America. It has been challenged by some who assert that political freedom is the sine qua non, whereas efforts to deal with economic and social issues may not be the business of the Jewish community relations field. Of course specifics must be analyzed carefully, but at the level of principle it is difficult to draw the line. The fabric of democratic practices in political, economic and social areas appears to be indivisible.

The forms of political democracy may be maintained in various countries as a propaganda device. Assertions of equal economic opportunity and of social egalitarianism can also be propagandistic. These are preserved as rituals in many countries around the world where people are not genuinely free to associate, to seek opportunity, and to choose their leaders. Only where the substance of all of these exists is there genuine democracy.

Real democracy flourishes where its processes inspire confidence that they can provide for the material needs as well as the political and personal freedoms of the people and that they can do so with justice and equity. Then the necessary constraints of the democratic process can be accepted, such as discussing public issues in an orderly and rational way, petitioning and appealing peaceably and without violence, complying with majority decisions and official regulations and judicial rulings.

When the democratic processes are perceived by significant segments of the people as failing to move the society toward economic security, social justice, and political equality, these constraints may be seen as unjust and oppressive. People who regard the democratic processes as unfair may be impelled to disregard the necessary constraints in seeking to assert their claims to a fair sharing in society's goods. The outward forms of political democracy alone will not protect against intergroup conflicts. Social and economic opportunity for all Americans must also be present.

20. Social Action

The Jewish community relations field engages in public action to expand opportunities and resources for all, regarding such action as essential to its efforts for the preservation of democratic processes.[34]

Discussion: Shortages in jobs, housing, health, and other services are conditions that tend to intensify discrimination and thus threaten to damage the effectiveness of American democratic processes. Therefore measures to broaden access to economic benefits and expand resources are proper concerns of the Jewish community relations program.

There have been controversies on the application of this principle. Differences of opinion exist within the Jewish community on the extent to which Jewish community relations agencies as such should become involved in broad programs for the public welfare. One school of thought would hold the community relations program directly to the areas where rights are diminished or threatened. But it follows from the preceding principles that the struggles for full facilities and for fair practices are interrelated, and must go on simultaneously. While the Jewish community relations agencies have a major responsibility to deal with those areas in which democratic rights are threatened or curtailed, they also have a broader responsibility to seek full employment, adequate housing, high-quality education, and sufficient services.

21. Government Responsibility

The Jewish community relations field, along with voluntary organizations representing other groups in the American mosaic, looks to and calls upon government at all levels to assume responsibilities as appropriate for the implementation of equal rights and opportunities.[35]

Discussion: The Jewish community relations agencies see as complementary their own voluntary efforts to serve democratic processes and the enlistment of the potent resources of government in the same struggle to maintain the American way of life. There is no inconsistency or contradiction between these approaches. At all levels, government is and should be responsive to the people, a pooling and extension of their individual and group power to achieve their just aims. Until quite recently, it would never have been regarded as controversial for voluntary agencies to call on the instrumentalities of government.

The Jewish community relations agencies are of course nonprofit, nonpartisan, nonpolitical organizations. All their activities through social action and interpretation to press government for any measure remain within the bounds defined by their tax-exempt, tax-deductible status. These include strict limitations on lobbying and absolute prohibition of participation in any way in electoral campaigns. Because of the importance of avoiding even the appearance of any link between the Jewish community and partisan politics, the NJCRAC has issued and periodically circulated

election guidelines.[36] These call upon Jewish leaders to refrain from using their present or past organizational identification when acting for or against any political candidate.
They also suggest that Jewish organizations avoid involvement in such electoral activities as awards to candidates and
use of letterhead or mailing list. But the guidelines are
explicit in pointing out that statements on public issues by
leaders or the organizations themselves are not under the
same constraints.

Not only have Jewish community relations agencies sought
to enlist the sanctions and resources of government at all
levels for enforcing nondiscrimination and ensuring full and
equal opportunity, but they have also supported efforts to
remove procedural barriers blocking desired substantive
action. Examples are Senate Rule XXII, the filibuster, and
the powers of the House Rules Committee; or, usually at the
state or local level, the gerrymandering of districts to reduce
the chances of fair representation of disadvantaged groups.

The expansion of government services to meet human
needs began during the Great Depression of the 1930s. It
had become evident that voluntary services, even if gener-
ously supported, were inadequate to maintain the social
fabric. State and municipal resources were also swamped.
Federal funding became imperative. Voluntary services have
not shrunk since then, but the magnitude of the needs has
increased. Today it seems impossible for voluntary services
to expand many times to meet the massive needs and to fill
the large gaps resulting from cutbacks in public services. It is
doubtful that states and localities losing federal funds can
adequately fill needs for necessary services. The "new federalism" places a very great strain on states, municipalities, and
voluntary philanthropy.

Since January 1981, the national administration has been
attempting to redefine the role of the federal and state
governments, on the assumption that there has been too
much governmental involvement and that people should
look more to voluntary efforts. It may be that some members
of the Jewish community will regard the previously unquestioned strategic principle of government responsibility as
requiring revision. Since at the level of principle there can be

no specification of which activities are appropriate for government, however, the controversy, if any, should be on the applications, and the principle itself can stand unchallenged.

The NJCRAC Joint Program Plan for 1981–82, adopted in April of 1981, deals with a number of matters concerning action by the federal government and by the states and municipalities, including among others the following: budgetary reductions, funding of health and social services, child welfare, block vs. categorical grants, aid to families with dependent children, food stamps, school lunches, the Comprehensive Training and Employment Act, Medicaid, housing and community development, legal services to the poor, voting rights, school desegregation, discrimination in housing, undocumented aliens, rights of women to choose abortion, the Constitutional Convention issue, and affirmative action.[37]

22. Women's Rights

Consonant with the promotion of equal opportunity and equal rights for all, the Jewish community relations field supports equal rights for women and the prohibition of arbitrary and unreasonable discrimination based on sex.[38]

Discussion: The issue of women's rights, endorsed without reservation by the Jewish community relations field, is resistive to the techniques that have been employed more successfully in other areas. Particularly thorough consideration is required, therefore, in devising appropriate and effective tactics for applying this unchallenged principle. Fortunately there are a number of well-informed women who are Jewish community relations leaders, and their participation, valuable in all areas of concern, is essential on this set of issues.

Among specific measures relating to this strategic principle that have been dealt with in NJCRAC Joint Program Plans are the Equal Rights Amendment, equal pay for equal work, opposition to sexual harassment and domestic violence, benefits for homemakers, and the right to choose abortion. Clearly, advocacy of women's rights rests on the principle of merit (see Number 24, below). Gains for women's rights advance general Jewish community relations objectives.

Since many people of all ethnic and economic groups are involved in the struggle for equal rights for women, this issue has exceptional importance for the coalition policy. Because in some respects it is a worldwide cause, it is also closely involved in questions regarding the United Nations and other international instrumentalities.

23. Affirmative Action

The Jewish community relations field believes that a just society has an obligation to seek to overcome the evils of past discrimination by affording special help to its victims and hastening their productive participation in the society.[39]

Discussion: This strategic principle addresses itself to one of the most heated issues of our time. The bitter struggle for civil rights—the spectacular days of sit-ins and marches and demonstrations and Supreme Court decisions and national figures on every television news program and murders and victories—culminated in the adoption of the Civil Rights Act of 1964. At that point, comfortable middle-class white Americans were ready for a respite.

But leaders of the black and other groups involved closely in the struggle, including many Jewish organizations, knew that the fight had just begun. As some black leaders said at the time, the door had been opened by the civil rights struggle, but now the people must be helped to walk through that door. Since then there has arisen among the groups that had suffered most from discrimination both a heightened level of aspiration because of legislative victories and a desperate frustration because hopes for true equality have not been realized. In the first flush of victory, it was not recognized how long and hard a road it would be, even with fair enforcement of civil rights laws. Other barriers to be surmounted were the heritage of poverty, unemployment, and underemployment; social and family disorganization; inadequate education, and even inadequate readiness for more education; entrapment in alcoholism, drug abuse, and criminality; exploitation by landlords and shopowners; police severity, and unequal treatment in the justice and corrections systems.

While there has been progress, implementation has been imperfect and advancement spotty. There have been spectacular achievements by a small proportion of blacks and members of other previously-discriminated-against groups. But the unequally distributed gains have generated complaints that class divisions have been accentuated, that only the new black middle class has advanced, and that a new black "underclass" has been created. The mood has turned sour in many respects. Lyndon B. Johnson, President at the time of the adoption of the Civil Rights Act, said: "Until we overcome unequal history, we cannot overcome unequal opportunity."

A just society has an obligation to seek to overcome the evils of past discrimination and other deprivations by special effort. If it fails to do so, our society will harbor inequality for generations, with attendant increases in intergroup hostility. Therefore the NJCRAC has endorsed the following:

a) Compensatory education, training, retraining, apprenticeship, job counseling and placement, financial assistance and other forms of help for the deprived and disadvantaged, to enable them as speedily as possible to realize their potential capabilities for participation in the main stream of American life. The sole criterion for eligibility for such special services must be individual need; the services must not be limited or offered preferentially on the basis of race, color, national origin, religion or sex.

b) Intensive recruitment of qualified and qualifiable individuals, utilizing not only traditional referral sources, but all those public and private resources that reach members of disadvantaged groups.

c) An ongoing review of established job and admissions requirements, including examinations and other selection methods, to make sure that they are performance-related and free of bias. . . .[40]

24. Merit

The Jewish community relations field regards merit as the touchstone of equality of opportunity.[41]

Discussion: This principle is unassailable. But how is merit to be determined? The NJCRAC statement on affirmative action indicates some of the complexities. The entire profession of psychology has been agitated by struggles over the use of psychological tests in schools and industries. Courts and regulatory bodies have ruled in some instances that widely used tests are inherently biased—a contention not accepted by many professional psychologists. The NJCRAC statement on affirmative action designates as "relevant in determining merit" such factors as poverty, cultural deprivation, inadequate schooling, discrimination or other deprivation, motivation, determination, perseverance, and resourcefulness.

On the other hand, quotas and proportional representation in hiring, upgrading, and admission are regarded as inconsistent with nondiscrimination and the goal of equal opportunity. The NJCRAC statement rejects quotas as "harmful in the long run to all." It calls on the government for vigorous enforcement of affirmative action programs, and equally for preventing abuses of such programs.

This principle and the preceding one (Numbers 24 and 23) are accepted only with trepidation in some sections of the Jewish community. People who get angry easily are tempted to oppose as "quotas" the entire effort to heal serious social ills through affirmative action. Groups still disadvantaged, on the other hand, complain bitterly of betrayal and abandonment by Jewish former allies. The principles themselves are nevertheless valid and necessary. They do require careful analysis in specific applications.

25. Balanced Program

The Jewish community relations field seeks the improvement of community relationships through a balanced program of social action and education.[42]

Discussion: The achievement of Jewish community relations aims is not a simple matter, and no single type of action can stand alone. Legislative measures, judicial enforcement and precedent, administrative regulation, petitions, the powers of municipal and state governments, pressures on officials and candidates, and other forms of social action must be supplemented by systematic education in the broad sense, including interreligious and intergroup contacts, education and school programs, use of the mass media of communication, and every other available tool.

Religious Freedom and Church-State Relationships

The Jewish community in the United States is both a religious and an ethnic group. There are other American religious groups (e.g., Armenian Orthodox) which have both a religious and an ethnic character, but most of them exist as entities only by virtue of a common religious identification. Jews, as do other religious groups in this country, look to the First Amendment, which bars governmental entanglement with religion and interference with religious freedom, as a fundamental bulwark of American democracy.

Long before the American Revolution, Roger Williams brought the idea of religious freedom to these shores, and it is now a basic aspect of our institutions. Because of the First Amendment, Jews and other religious groups have been able to flourish as equals in this country, and to maintain their beliefs and practice their traditions. This is in contrast to the many nations, today and in the past, where groups dissenting from an established religion could exist only on sufferance. Fortunately, few nontotalitarian nations today practice religious oppression. Jews may observe their religion securely in democratic countries even if for reasons of history these retain an official religion (as in England). The protection of the First Amendment is nevertheless greatly to be cherished.

In further elucidation of the broad policies, especially those regarding democratic pluralism and the American way, Jewish community relations agencies have outlined the following principles for the preservation of religious freedom.

26. State and Religion

The Jewish community relations field believes that democracy in the United States is in large measure a product of the unique principle in our basic law that keeps religion outside the jurisdiction of the state.[43]

Discussion: Religion has always been and continues to be the central core of Jewish life, in this country and throughout the world.

The American democratic system is founded in large part upon ethical and moral principles derived from the great religions of mankind. The preservation and fostering of these concepts are essential to the fullest realization of the American Creed. Their growth and development as major forces in American life should be the deep concern of every citizen.

Religious liberty is an indispensable aspect of democratic freedom. As a nation of people attached to many different religious faiths, or to none, we owe our survival to the universal acceptance of the uniquely American concept that the relationship between man and God is not and may not be subject to governmental control or regulation. Any impairment of that principle threatens religious liberty and brings other basic freedoms into jeopardy.

Today throughout the world there is a great upsurge of religious feeling, unfortunately often accompanied in many places by fanaticism and hostility to those who believe or practice differently. In Iran, a form of Islamic fundamentalism is engaged in persecution of the Bahais, and the fate of other non-Moslem groups is still unknown. Egypt is torn by struggles between Moslems and Coptic Christians. The conflict in Northern Ireland is based in large part on religious identity. Lebanon is a shattered society, with little peace and mutual acceptance among a large number of sects. In this country, while fanaticism has been kept within bounds by the universal respect religious groups have for the Constitution, there are evidences of disturbing tendencies toward rejection of religious pluralism.

This strategic principle is unquestioned in the Jewish community. In American society today, however, it is obviously under direct attack.

27. The Public Schools and Religion

The Jewish community relations field regards the maintenance and furtherance of religion as responsibilities of the synagogue, the church, and the home, and not of the public school system.[44]

Discussion: This means that the utilization in any manner of the time, facilities, personnel, or funds of the public school system for purposes of religious instruction should not be permitted.

The schools are the battleground today where some of the first skirmishes in the campaign to limit religious freedom are being fought. Prayers, Bible teaching, and scientific creationism are among the heated issues in many school districts. The close connection between these issues and the fundamental American democratic protections is underlined by the proposed Helms Prayer Amendment, which would alter the First Amendment to the Constitution.

The public schools must recognize the realities of religious differences in the community among their pupils. They should continue to teach pupils that acceptance and respect for such differences are basic to American democracy and contribute toward harmonious living in a free society.

In teaching morality, ethics, and good citizenship, the public schools must not seek or assign theological sanctions for the values they attempt to inculcate in the children of our heterogeneous population. The public schools must and should teach with all possible objectivty the role that religions and their doctrines and sacred books, including the Bible, have played in the life of mankind and the development of society. But such instruction in the public schools must not, in the guise of teaching about religions, actually be covert religious instruction, either sectarian or "religion-in-general." Religious instruction isolates and demeans children of minority religions, such as Jews. The effort to extract a "common core" can only lead to a watering down of all that is meaningful in every religious faith, while harmfully granting to a governmental body the power to select among religious tenets.

In accordance with this strategic principle, Jewish community relations agencies have opposed the use of public school premises during school hours for religious education, meetings, or worship; the reading or recitation of prayers; the reading of the Bible (except as included in a course in literature); the distribution of Bibles or religious tracts; the singing of religious hymns; the granting of school credits for religious studies; the wearing of any type of clerical garb by public school teachers on school premises; the holding of public school classes on the premises of religious institutions; the taking of a religious census of pupils; the observance of religious festivals in the public elementary and high school, including joint observances such as Christmas-Hanukkah and Easter-Passover (but if there are nevertheless such observances, Jewish children should have the right to refrain from participation); released-time or dismissal-time programs (with a number of qualifications); and the inclusion of religious elements in high school graduation exercises.

On the question of governmental aid to schools under religious control, through direct subsidies of funds or supplies or services, such as transportation and textbooks, or indirectly by tax credits and vouchers, there is division in the Jewish community. While some regard these as contrary to the separation principle, others disagree; obviously application of the strategic principle, which all accept, requires careful analysis and thought in this area. No one opposes the use of such schools for the provision of lunches, or of medical and dental services to children.

Another area where there is need for detailed analysis is the closing of public schools on Jewish High Holy Days (which most regard as purely a matter for administrative decision by school authorities).

28. Sensitive Issues

Because of the unusual sensitivity of issues concerning religion and the schools, the Jewish community relations field emphasizes the need for care in planning action, since unwise and poorly timed measures may intensify community relations problems without producing any positive results.[45]

Discussion: Few Americans can be found who would deny the value of religious freedom for all. Paradoxically, however, many utterly innocuous efforts to seek modification of Christian holiday observances or other injections of religion into the public schools, whether by Jews or other minority religious groups, have evoked storms of outrage and bigotry. This has been particularly true in largely homogeneous suburbs, small towns, and rural areas. How, the indignant parents ask, can anyone object to a beautiful Christmas pageant? To starting the day with a prayer? To reading a Bible passage every day? Some may then go beyond outrage and charge a plot by the Jewish radicals to subvert the morals of their children. This pattern of conflict has recurred with dismaying frequency.

Especially in more or less isolated and religiously homogeneous communities, there are good people who uphold the Constitution but are so steeped in their own religious tradition that they cannot conceive that their practices might give offense to anyone. They have never had to face up to the idea that people brought up in another tradition can also become decent, moral citizens. Their panicky outrage reflects their fear that, along with their own cherished beliefs, the very foundations of the nation and of morality are under attack.

The Synagogue Council of America and the NJCRAC have been at great pains to explain that the foregoing principle of opposition to religion in the schools (Number 27) does not mean a declaration of war or the opening of a free-fire zone. They offer and recommend consultation before any public action is taken in this delicate area.

Before a Jewish group initiates action, there must be preparation, including interpretation within the Jewish community and informal conferences with educational administrators, clergy, and the like. Timing, preparation, and manner of negotiations are crucial. Calm negotiations on a wide range of issues, in the absence of a specific complaint, may bring progressively favorable results without concomitant tensions or hostility. Negotiations with school administrators are best carried on without publicity or direct public involvement. If the atmosphere is propitious, broader dialogues can be attempted.

It is much better to negotiate about school practices in a quiet period, rather than after controversy has aroused strong emotional stands. Whenever possible, negotiations regarding Christmas or Easter observances should be initiated at times remote from the holidays. Year-round education, and relationships on a number of issues, are important.

In the course of protracted calm negotiations, Jewish community representatives may find it desirable to agree to compromises that bring some improvement. If they do, they must make clear that they still adhere to the policy of opposition to all religious practices or observances in the schools. Whatever the school's policies may be, monitoring is necessary, because individual teachers or new administrators may institute less-desirable practices after years without problems.

Because some injections of religion into the public schools may actually violate existing laws (although the parents may not realize it), lawsuits may be initiated under some circumstances. Litigation is wisely regarded as a last resort, to be turned to after other efforts—education, persuasion, negotiation—have failed or been rejected. Litigation, when well planned, can result in wide-ranging rulings by the courts, and even the Supreme Court, clarifying the application of the constitutional protection of religious freedom. Short of actual litigation, it has sometimes been found useful to seek rulings from attorneys general, state education departments, or other officials.

29. Religion and Public Policy

The Jewish community relations field holds it to be an impairment of religious liberty if any person is penalized for adhering to his or her religious beliefs, or not adhering to any religious belief, so long as he or she does not interfere with the rights of others or endanger the public peace or security.[46]

Discussion: The public schools are not the only settings in which church-state relationships may be involved. Some of the same considerations as in the two preceding strategic principles regarding the public schools (Numbers 27 and 28) apply also to other institutions. It must be recognized that all church-state issues are very sensitive.

The Jewish community is not a minority religious group protesting inequities and beseeching equal protection. It is one of the many co-equal groups comprising the pluralistic American society, all seeking to advance the dynamic growth of that society in democratic directions. Among the public policy concerns that have been addressed by Jewish community relations programs are the following: Sunday observance laws, religious symbols on public property, the question of religion in the U.S. Census, the Prayer Amendment, conflicts of schedules with Jewish religious holidays and with the Sabbath—including primaries, elections, civil service examinations, etc.

What all these matters have in common among themselves and with the questions of religion and the public schools is that they involve governments or agencies sponsored or financed by governments at the federal, state, or local level. Their functions and operations are thus to some extent defined by law. In recent years the reach of the law has been extended, as the distinction between public and voluntary institutions has been blurred by partial public funding.

Beyond these, there is a much more extensive body of Jewish–non-Jewish relationships, formal and informal, that are not mediated through public instrumentalities. The following strategic principles deal with such interreligious and intergroup relationships.

Interreligious and Intergroup Relation- ships

Both as a religious and as an ethnic group, the Jewish community is involved in a bewildering variety of informal relationships in the pluralistic American society.

Jews are numerically few in comparison with adherents of a number of the major Christian denominations in this country. A very frequent practice, nevertheless, has been the balancing of one Roman Catholic, one Protestant, and one Jewish speaker at all kinds of celebrations, rallies, and events. This tripartite division has in some ways been of positive value, as a public recognition of religious pluralism and of the acceptance of Jews in American life. There have also been interreligious complications and misunderstandings, because Judaism, unlike many Christian denominations, is not exclusively a belief-system, but also a tradition and a way of life. Christian clergymen are sometimes baffled by the lack of distinction in Jewish life between "religious" and "secular."

As an ethnic group, the Jewish community enters into relationships with a variety of groups on the American scene, so-called minorities (i.e., blacks, Hispanics, Orientals, Native Americans), so-called ethnics (i.e., second- or third-generation American Irish, Poles, Italians, etc.), and different kinds of functional groups—trade unions, professional and business associations, civic bodies, etc.

Some of the day-by-day interreligious contacts are of a formal nature, such as conferences in which representatives of the Synagogue Council participate along with delegations from the National Council of Churches and the United States Catholic Conference, or local events sponsored by several congregations, Jewish and Christian. The same kinds of formal contacts occur in general intergroup relations, as, for instance, participation of Jewish and non-Jewish organizations in a conference on health care or child welfare. Studies, documents, and programs developed in formal interreligious and intergroup cooperative efforts have been valuable in dealing with a wide range of questions.

The overwhelming bulk of interreligious and intergroup contacts are of an informal nature, person to person. In schools, on the job, in neighborhoods, at recreational facilities, people of all religions and groups may have meaningful associations with each other. Even though people of like group tend to cluster in little occupational or residential enclaves, changed circumstances and legal requirements have in any case eliminated some forms of exclusiveness. Thus, the occasions for natural interreligious and intergroup associations are very numerous. While people are not necessarily identified by group, in a large proportion of continuing contacts group membership is known. Informal associations are thus very important factors, for good or ill, in affecting interreligious and intergroup relationships in this country.

Of course there is frequent conflict among all the different kinds of groups, and alignments and coalitions are constantly shifting. A number of strategic principles have nevertheless been developed in the Jewish community relations program for maintaining amicable interreligious and intergroup relationships, which transcend the divergences on specific issues.

30. Mutual Respect

The Jewish community relations field seeks to foster intergroup understanding by creating a climate in which groups, and individuals identified with groups, can develop their fullest potentials in their distinctive ways, rather than by having to deny or minimize group differences.[47]

Discussion: Both diversity and unity are needed in American life. The value of differences must be recognized, so that contacts can be utilized for favorable outcomes. The right to be different carries as its obverse the responsibility to preserve the essential unity of American life. In view of the many segregating tendencies, a key problem is to promote associations that cement relationships and, at the same time, honor and promote regard for group differences.

Durable bridges between groups can best be built if the groups themselves provide secure foundations. A person who has grown up with a firm sense of security and identification within his or her own group is usually able to understand the group identifications of others.

31. Intergroup Conflicts

The Jewish community relations field seeks ways for all groups to live together harmoniously, despite the existence of intergroup differences on doctrines or public issues.[48]

Discussion: This principle is not generally questioned. However, its implementation requires considerable sophistication, because it is necessary to distinguish between a specific doctrine (e.g., original sin) or position (e.g., black pressures for quotas to advance affirmative action) and the possibilities for a wide variety of productive contacts with the group and its members. When differences arise, these should be faced frankly.

From time to time there have been candid mutual explorations of differences on a variety of issues by Catholic, Protestant, and Jewish spokesmen or representatives. These "dialogues" have most often dealt with public issues, such as religion and public education, rather than with doctrinal differences. While these have not greatly modified positions, mutual attitudes have been improved by interchange of views. The principal value has been the substitution of rational examination of differences for acrimonious exchanges of accusations and polemics. Thus violently hostile controversy has been averted while differences have been faced directly.

There have been a small number of informal conferences of black and Jewish leadership to talk out differences. One instance followed the dismissal of Andrew Young as ambassador to the United Nations for covert contacts with representatives of the Palestine Liberation Organization, which some black leaders mistakenly ascribed to pressure by Jewish agencies.

Social conflict is an aspect of democratic living. The goal of community relations can never be the development of a situation in which conflict is completely absent, but rather a society of individuals who can resolve conflicts through acceptance of differences.

32. Prejudice and Stereotypes

The Jewish community relations field combats intergroup tension and hostility by seeking to deal with attitudes, prejudices, and stereotypes.[49]

Discussion: Differences of doctrine and conflicts over public issues may be sufficiently rational to be faced directly and discussed frankly. Other sources of tension and intergroup hostility, however, such as prejudices and stereotypes, reflect attitudes that are only partly accessible to rational discussion. They represent stubborn and deep-seated problems. The greedy Jew, the lazy black, the inscrutable Oriental—such stereotypes are familiar because they are encountered so frequently. No such ascription of characteristics broadside to a whole group can be helpful in community relations. Even if accompanied by less unfavorable attributes—e.g., the Jew is clever, the black is musically talented—they are still stereotypes.

In the 1940s, the Jewish agencies conducted a great deal of research to determine the sources of such hostile attitudes. More recently, the practice has been to fund or assist academic institutions and research institutes to conduct additional studies on this question, and of course there has been extensive research not stemming from stimulation by the Jewish community.

As might have been expected, no single or simple answer could be found. Prejudice is not always the same. There is multiple determination. It differs according to the groups involved, the character of the prejudiced person, the object of prejudice, and the situation. Among the factors are traditional group and family attitudes, childhood teaching, atmosphere of the early home, character formation in the family milieu, personal quirks, associates, life problems and relationships in adult life, misinterpreted actualities, and exposure to propaganda and instigation. In addition, the time cycle and direction of causation are by no means clear; tensions engender prejudices as much as prejudices engender tensions, in continuous reciprocal influence.

The implications for action of these complex findings are equally varied. While there can obviously be no absolute cure for prejudice, there are numerous avenues for action that may have validity under certain circumstances. The following strategic principles (Numbers 33 through 46) deal with some of the approaches that can be utilized. Two of the principal instrumentalities, the schools (Numbers 37 through 40) and the mass media of communication (Numbers 41 through 46), will receive more extended treatment in the following sections.

33. Dispelling Misinformation

Imparting correct information is an instrumentality of the Jewish community relations field for combating stereotypes and prejudice.[50]

Discussion: There is a great deal of misinformation being distributed by anti-Semitic or just plain ignorantly bigoted groups. It is therefore necessary to have on hand factual and interpretive materials about Jews and Judaism. Although a document may be unable to change attitudes by itself, it can be essential as supplement or follow-up to forms of programming with more personal involvement of the misinformed. The preparation and adaptation of such materials and their constant improvement are therefore valuable aids to the community relations program.

Some misstatements find their way into textbooks and other materials distributed as information. Complementing efforts to produce and use accurate information, there is need for a continuous process of monitoring texts and similar ostensibly factual materials.

While sometimes practical, this strategic principle is difficult to apply. The reason is that attitudes and ways of thinking about people are, in general, more important in molding intergroup relations than factual information or misinformation. Supplying accurate information to people is not enough to eliminate prejudice or correct discrimination, since people usually find ways to protect deep-seated beliefs even in the face of evidence to the contrary. To be effective, the information must be received, perceived, and accepted— not an easy outcome to achieve.

34. Equal-Status Contacts

The Jewish community relations field fosters good intergroup relations by bringing people from different groups together in natural, equal-status contacts.[51]

Discussion: There is no adequate substitute for such actual personal association. But mingling, by itself, does not guarantee a constructive outcome and may produce boomerang effects, such as magnifying differences and reinforcing existing prejudicial attitudes. Careful preparation of contacts is necessary, to ensure an easy, natural situation and genuine acceptance of equal status.

There's the rub! While the validity of this strategic principle is clear, in practical application it is not easy to assure truly equal-status contacts on a natural basis. The difficulty reflects principally the slow progress that has been made toward integration of neighborhoods. Many areas and suburbs are still not merely all-white or all-black, but all–Irish Catholic or all–old settler–American–Episcoplian or all-Jewish. Separation in neighborhoods means separation in schools, stores, bars, and in almost every other setting where natural person-to-person adult contacts can take place except in colleges and at work, where the problems still exist but have been slightly mitigated. As the Hawley studies show, desegregation of schools even by court order does work, but slowly and with many problems.[52]

Formal contacts of group leaders and organizational representatives are much easier to achieve than natural informal person-to-person intergroup contacts on an equal-status basis. They can have considerable value, since the participating leaders may help mold opinion within their own groups. Public activities of an intergroup nature may be reported in the specialized media (black, denominational, etc.), and therefore the leadership contacts, if successful, can reach the general membership of the groups.

Person-to-person contacts can also be fostered in groups drawn from a number of neighborhoods, such as unions, veterans organizations, churches, and PTAs in mixed schools. Sports and recreational centers may also be helpful. Too frequently, though, intergroup differences may be carried into these settings and tensions can be exacerbated, especially where the contacts are episodic and there is not enough continuity for people to become acquainted.

A special form of contact has been mediated through intersectarian organizations, such as the National Conference of Christians and Jews. Although there has been a tendency for such interdenominational bodies to sink to the level of the least common denominator and to substitute exhortations of good will for program, they can represent valuable resources for cooperation on the basis of complete acceptance and frank facing of differences.

35. The Law and the Reduction of Prejudice

The Jewish community relations field looks to the law, as the embodiment of the society's standards, to advance equality not only by its coercive powers but also through moral force going beyond its sanctions.[53]

Discussion: Prejudices are hostile attitudes with deep roots. Of course no one maintains that prejudices can be made to disappear simply by passing a law against them. They are internal, and their origins are too complex.

This strategic principle relates specifically to the impact of the law on intergroup attitudes and practices. The law is here defined as the exertion of governmental power, whether in the form of a statute, a judgment of a court, or an order or act of an administrative agency or official. The principle rests upon the assumption, unfortunately not always realized in practice, that the law and its enforcement through the justice system not only are fair but are perceived to be fair to all groups in the community. To the extent that justice is or is regarded as biased for or against any group or groups, the application of this principle would require earnest and urgent attention to correct that situation.

In this nation founded upon democratic principles, the instrumentalities of the law presumably are accessible to the people for promoting the general welfare. Our system of government should permit us to look to the law with confidence as an expression of the popular will. Hence laws can be accepted as guides to conduct.

Legislation and legal rulings defining and broadening human rights have had a highly beneficial effect. Law tends to become recognized as the community standard, including the legal enactments designed to advance the American Creed. Since most people are law-abiding, their behavior tends to conform to the community standards embodied in the law, even if their own attitudes were originally in conflict with the statute when it was proposed. When the law clearly frowns upon discrimination, those who are not prejudiced are strengthened in their ability to practice nondiscrimination, and even the prejudiced are likely to conform. When a person stops discriminating, even if only to conform to the law, the change in behavior automatically encourages the adoption of less-biased attitudes. This is a potent force for reduction of prejudice.

Heated community conflicts have occurred at times of changes in law, or rulings about the application of the law, regarding, for instance, integration of schools (particularly busing), zoning law changes, and redrawing of voting district lines. While intergroup clashes are conspicuous and tend to be publicized, on innumerable occasions there are improvements with no noisy struggle. These were not sensational and hence never made the news media. Care in ensuring that the law and justice system are fair can help defuse the likelihood of challenges to the moral authority of the law. Intergroup participation in planning and monitoring frequently leads to both fairness in fact and community acceptance.

36. Common Action

The Jewish community relations field believes cooperation of groups for common goals to be especially effective in reducing hostility and prejudice.[54]

Discussion: The most effective approach by far to the improvement of intergroup attitudes is that of finding ways for religious, ethnic, or other groups to work together for common objectives in the improvement of the general welfare. Hostility tends to give way to the spirit of cooperation that is engendered in the joint striving for shared goals.

This strategic principle is the complement of the policy of coalition (Number 8). It indicates that coalition is not only likely to be more effective, but that it also brings the indirect benefits of reduction of tensions and prejudices. As in all coalition situations, it is necessary to recognize and make allowances for the reality of differences on some issues, while cooperating for those goals which are held in common.

Regardless of the effect of differences in dogma and practice, most of the major religious bodies share many civic and social goals, such as on questions of immigration and civil rights. Many church-related but independent bodies have been created to deal with major civic questions and areas of interest. In the pursuit of shared aims, joint participation has had a beneficial effect and has lessened tensions arising from frankly acknowledged differences over other social issues.

Any community relations program of intergroup activities aimed at achieving the goal of more harmonious living together in America must place particular emphasis on cooperative social action. Jewish organizations share many common goals with ethnic, veterans, labor, academic, women's, and civic groups, as well as other religious bodies. Because of its double benefits—goal-effectiveness and improved intergroup relationships—this strategic principle is basic in meeting a wide variety of situations.

Education and the Schools

In the earlier days when most American Jews were immigrants or first-generation Americans, they were devoted supporters of the public school system. They saw it as their ladder to success. Today, however, many Jews are dismayed by the problems affecting the public schools, as are people in all groups. Many Jewish parents feel that the public schools have not met their insistent demand for quality. They fear the turbulence that has accompanied efforts to meet the problems of the disadvantaged.

Some have turned to private education, either Jewish day schools which foster Jewish identity, or other nonpublic schools which presumably offer the benefits of quality education. The majority of Jewish children, however, like the children of all groups in American society, continue to rely on public education.

Community relations issues have arisen in the elementary and secondary schools in connection with such matters as integration, quality education for all pupils, decentralization, community control, equal opportunity, presentation in the curriculum of the pluralistic character of American life, and intergroup conflict among students.

The nurturing of sound intergroup attitudes among children, in private as well as public schools, has both immediate and long-range values. Children are participating members of society in their own right. It is assumed also that the development of realistic attitudes toward intergroup differences in American life among children will carry over into adult life, and will contribute to mature interrelationships in our society.

The Jewish community relations agencies have maintained extensive programs involving contact with the schools. These programs have been directed toward advancing equality and assuring high-quality education. Since for the country as a whole these goals must be sought chiefly through the public school system, the Jewish community relations program has been concerned with maintaining the viability of the public schools. The pursuit of these aims has been guided by the following strategic principles.

37. Centrality of the Public Schools

The Jewish community relations field regards the public schools as the cornerstone of the American democratic system, deserving the full support of the American people.[55]

Discussion: Whatever the value of private education, it is the public school system that will continue for the indefinite future to receive and to educate the great majority of American children. Parents should be free, on a voluntary basis, to seek any legitimate form of education that they may wish for their children, in religion-oriented or other private schools. Concern with public education is an inherent aspect of concern with the future of American society.

There is a reciprocal interplay between the problems of the public schools and the crises of American society generally. The difficulties of the schools, and especially of the inner-city schools, cannot be solved entirely within the public school system, as though there were no interaction with the larger society. Not only teachers, parents, students, school administrators, and board members, but all who have some effective role to play in modern society—taxpayers, public officials, civic leaders, newspapers and all the media—must contribute to the improvement of the public schools. The schools must be enabled to respond affirmatively to new problems and prove receptive and sensitive to the needs and opinions of young people.

The weaknesses of the public schools have been criticized justly. In addition, the schools have become increasingly the targets of destructive attacks, by frustrated and in some instances misguided Americans, some of whom seem to be ignorant or contemptuous of democratic processes. While the public schools may be challenged as never before, it is unwarranted to charge that they have failed. Americans concerned for our democratic processes should be wary of joining in the persistent denigration of the public school system.

38. The Schools and Equality

The Jewish community relations field sees quality integrated education and equal educational opportunity as top-priority goals of American education.[56]

Discussion: The three principal aims of education are educational excellence, self-development, and social responsibility. Integration is essential in the pursuit of the goals of education. It is not a separate aim in itself but an aspect of quality education for all children. Schools make a significant contribution to better intergroup relationships among children when they provide a sound and democratic classroom climate, and when they draw children from diversified rather than homogeneous areas. Schools must integrate their faculties and keep classes from becoming so large as to exacerbate possible tensions.

Specific positive measures that public schools can take include:

- revision of school-district boundaries for greater balance, and assigning children, by busing or other means as indicated, to schools where they can participate in a constructive integrated educational experience
- pairing of existing schools and use of magnet schools
- selecting sites for new schools so as to draw upon multi-ethnic pupil populations.

These need not provoke "white flight" if continued quality is assured. The persistence of de facto segregation based on discriminatory housing patterns is a problem of particular urgency today, and obviously requires broader action than is possible within the control of a school system.

Demands for decentralization and community control of public schools have been pressed in some metropolitan areas to improve the quality of education for blacks, Hispanics, and other disadvantaged groups. People who despair of progress toward integration and more equal education seek community control. While the Jewish community relations agencies believe that community involvement in the schools is desirable, the sloganized use of "decentralization" and "community control" is not regarded as constructive. Such slogans prolong intergroup fragmentation and block necessary integration.

It has also been contended that only members of the disadvantaged groups themselves really understand the needs of their children and care enough to teach them effectively. The Jewish community relations agencies believe that group membership may be a relevant consideration under some circumstances but should never be the exclusive criterion in the selection of teachers. All who see the public schools as a vital factor for American democratic pluralism should seek higher status for all teachers, fair employment and advancement policies on the basis of genuine merit, more equitable salaries, assurance of tenure, opportunities for paraprofessionals to train to be full-fledged teachers, and viable pension arrangements. These are promising approaches to quality teaching for all students.

39. Intergroup Education

The Jewish community relations field fosters efforts by schools, public and private, to increase intergroup contacts and understanding among children.[57]

Discussion: Intergroup education programs within the schools have varied widely, reflecting differences in educational philosophy, the specific needs and resources and composition of the community and the school population, grade levels, etc. In some cases programs have emphasized factual information about different groups in the United States, their history and customs. There has also been much programming aimed at the inculcation of attitudes and opinions, teaching the meaning of democracy, and the need for mutual acceptance. The meaning of the Bill of Rights is a topic in most American schools. The consequences in human suffering of totalitarian regimes, as in Nazi Germany, are presented to many American school children.

In some instances the human relations content has been integrated with the general school curriculum, rather than taught as a special subject. Particularly through social studies courses and the selection of literature for English courses, the process of intergroup education has penetrated and become identified with every aspect of the school program. Extracurricular activities have also been useful.

The maintenance of a democratic atmosphere within the school is also a basic formative factor in good intergroup relations. The equal and accepted participation in school activities of teachers of all groups is in itself a valuable experience. As an extension of this approach, the school can make a great contribution to intergroup relations by providing a warm, accepting atmosphere that promotes wholesome growth to emotional maturity.

While the public school system has been the principal resource for intergroup education of children, parochial and other nonpublic schools have also undertaken constructive programs.

In addition to programs conducted within the schools, many activities have been directed to young people through PTAs, teacher and educational associations, and teacher-training institutions. Thus adults may also benefit from these programs. Many youth-serving agencies other than the schools have conducted similar intergroup-relations programs, including both church-connected and non-church-connected youth groups, institutes, centers, and camps.

Successful intergroup education is possible only when educational facilities are adequate. Crowded classrooms, poor teachers, inadequate curricula, and authoritarian methods all militate against learning. Effective intergroup education requires commitment on the part of all school personnel, administrators, supervisors, and teachers. The schools must be open to innovation; for instance, early-childhood education, such as Head Start, has effectively involved parents as well as children from a variety of groups in the community. Only schools that are not substandard can engage in programs of intergroup education that are not themselves substandard.

Despite problems and pitfalls, this strategic principle, of fostering intergroup understanding through the schools, is universally accepted. It has been applied in a great variety of ways in different situations.

40. Financing the Public Schools

While recognizing that the deficiencies of many public schools are real and by no means exclusively financial, the Jewish community relations field regards adequate financing of the public schools as imperative.[58]

Discussion: This principle is not specific in its application, but it may seem to run counter to trends in public financing today. The idea that "you can't solve problems by throwing money at them" is the prevailing philosophy, at least with regard to non-military services. (The superintendent of a large city public school system replied to this slogan: "Maybe so, but I'd like to try it with money some time.") Throughout the country, there are pressures to cut public school budgets in the face of more complex needs and rising costs. In the many areas where school budgets must be adopted by local vote, it is difficult to get taxpayers to endorse even skeleton budgets. Financial problems are particularly severe for the inner-city schools, which are called upon to cope with violence, drugs, and general turbulence, reflecting inadequate health and mental health care, miserable housing conditions, and a dismal quality of life.

The population of school-age children is declining in many districts. It has been possible to accommodate to today's approaches to federal finances and public expenditures only because there are fewer children to be taught. The tax base of cities and local government units, resting upon regressive property taxes, is plainly inadequate, and overreliance upon it results in inequities. Taxpayer resistance spawned Proposition 13 in California, Proposition 2 1/2 in Massachusetts, and similar hobbling measures in other states. Yet federal and state financing are also being tightened. State aid is limited by the domination of many legislatures by rural and suburban representatives unsympathetic to the inner cities.

Equity in sharing is necessary. It has been suggested that an appropriate rule of thumb would be to provide one-third of public school funds from local, one-third from state, and one-third from federal sources. But the adequacy of the total sum provided is even more important than the equity of the sharing.

Meanwhile, the proposal to dismantle the federal Department of Education is a significant indicator of the rejection by Washington of further involvement at the national level in the financing of local school systems. The "new federalism" means reduced grants to states. Proposals for voucher payments, or tax credits for parents of non-public-school pupils, would have the effect of draining additional amounts from a shrinking pool of funds available for public education. The result would be further deterioration. This strategic principle asserts that it is necessary, in the cause of good community relations, for Jewish agencies and individuals to express themselves vigorously regarding the financial needs of public education.

The Mass Media of Communication

The mass media of communication touch every aspect of society in America today. Their impact upon personal and public life is so great as to be incalculable. The question for the Jewish community relations agencies is not whether to use the mass media—it would be impossible to do without them—but rather for what specific purposes, in what ways, and what their role should be in the total program.

The term "mass media" designates those means of communication which are addressed to the public generally. Examples are television, radio, newspapers, books, pamphlets, leaflets, magazines, advertisements, posters, displays, recordings, the stage, parades, rallies, lectures, motion pictures, and film strips. The same media may be used to reach special groups, such as ethnic or professional groups. Since neither the media nor their audiences are undifferentiated, their community relations import reflects what media are being used, for what purpose, and for what audience.

Jewish community relations purposes include both the planned use of the media for the achievement of positive goals and the effort to counteract uses considered to be antagonistic or harmful to good community interrelations. Both the communications produced specifically for their intergroup effort and the mainstream, a vastly greater

79

amount, are of concern to the Jewish community relations program.

The earlier uses of the mass media for Jewish community relations purposes were designed to refute canards, defamation, rumors, and stereotypes, and to advocate intergroup harmony and good will. In the middle 1930s, to meet the rising menace of Hitlerism, pamphlets and other mass media were used to expose Nazism, explode racial myths, and identify and isolate American Nazi sympathizers. In this period, there was virtually unquestioning acceptance of the power of the mass media.

During the late 1940s and early 1950s there was a searching examination of the appropriate place of the mass media in Jewish community relations work. Some of the agencies initiated programs of scientific research to evaluate their approaches. The period of criticism and reappraisal brought substantial agreement that, while unwise use of the mass media can result in waste and even damage, when properly used the media constitute a powerful and essential tool. Skilled use is most important, since the impact of any message is materially affected by its content, the particular medium through which it is conveyed, the manner of its presentation, and the ways in which different groups perceive it.[59]

The following strategic principles have been developed to serve as guidelines in the use of the media for community relations purposes.

41. Goals of Mass Communication

The Jewish community relations field employs the mass media for concrete, specific goals rather than for general promotion of goodwill or other unspecific aims.[60]

Discussion: Human-relations objectives cannot be promoted or sold in the same way as commercial products. Some advertising techniques have been employed successfully to promote one of a number of competing brands of a product already accepted as a commodity (e.g., soap or toothpaste). These include mechanical repetition, substitution of fantasy for reality, romantic claims, and status striving. Experience shows that when applied to community relations themes, these techniques can lead at best to superficial verbal acceptance. There may be no follow-through to any action of value.

Mass media have been used successfully for two major community relations purposes: conveying accurate information and inducing desirable social action. Both require presentation in as concrete and specific a form as possible. Prior to the civil rights legislation of the 1960s, it was necessary to bring the facts of discrimination to large segments of the American people whose own lives were not sufficiently touched by it to be sensitive to its effects. The information brought about an awakening of the American consciousness. After the facts were more widely recognized, specific interpretation of legislative proposals through the media helped mobilize concrete action.

For less-specific community relations goals, such as eliminating prejudice and creating a climate of opinion favorable to equality, the evidence suggests that these are most effectively sought over the long run by social action and the cumulative effect of specific communications.

42. Targeting

The Jewish community relations field addresses communications to specific target audiences, each in terms of its own identifications, wants, and needs.[61]

Discussion: For maximum effectiveness, messages are targeted to specific groups, such as business, labor, veterans, adolescents, etc. Each group responds in characteristic ways to the various media and themes. It is self-defeating to try to simplify a message to the least common denominator in an effort to gain wider attention and appeal.

Messages sponsored by clearly disinterested public figures, or by leaders of the group to whom the message is addressed, can-receive widespread acceptance. Since Jewish community relations agencies are involved with such leadership in day-by-day intergroup cooperation for civic improvement, their endorsement of communications can frequently be obtained. When these messages then appear in newspapers or on television and radio, they gain more attention and credence because of their indirect approach and lack of self-interested sponsorship. In some situations, however, it is advisable or appropriate to issue a communication in the name of a Jewish organization or a number of them, in order to inform the public of the Jewish agency's sponsorship or participation in a project contributing to community welfare.

The effectiveness of communications through the mass media is greatly increased by various forms of follow-up, such as in face-to-face discussion groups. Communications addressed to opinion molders (such as clergymen, union officials, teachers, civic leaders) have particular importance, because they may then be transmitted by word of mouth, with added authority because of the sponsorship of the respected opinion leader.

43. Content of Communication

The Jewish community relations agencies address the interests and beliefs that the members of the target audience already recognize and hold, rather than attempting to alter their basic concepts.[62]

Discussion: This is a fundamental and accepted strategic principle, but it may be elusive in practical application. It is much easier for a communicator to know what he would like to say than it is to imagine how it will sound in the ears of the recipient, and in the heat of action this analysis may be overlooked. That is why advertisers usually pretest their messages, and even then mistakes sometimes occur—as when the Chevrolet people couldn't sell the Chevy Nova to Hispanics, who read it "No va!" ("It won't go!")

Communications that identify with people's specific needs for recognition, advancement, self-respect, and such values as patriotism and honor are more readily accepted than those which are perceived, for however unlikely a reason, as challenging or disparaging these values. Messages that attempt reversals of the ongoing interests of major groups in the American public, or that seem to be expressions of narrow or partisan concerns, may boomerang.

Every audience consists of individuals who perceive messages by associating them with previous ideas and predispositions. Thus messages of any sort are most likely to reinforce prior convictions or stimulate action among those already convinced. Feeling patterns themselves are rarely modified by messages in the media, even with repeated exposure.

To maximize positive effects and minimize the danger of possible resentment and backfire, messages should be short, direct, and as simple and uncomplicated as possible. Low-key messages are less likely to provoke negative reactions than those that are perceived as high-pressure or emotional in tone.

44. Differential Impact of Media

In utilizing the various media, the Jewish community relations field takes into consideration their differences in audience and reception.[63]

Discussion: Those media concerned primarily with the dissemination of current news, such as newspapers, weekly magazines, and television and radio news broadcasts, are best adapted to messages aimed at immediate actions, such as legislative interpretation. Petitions and rallies also promote specific actions. On the other hand, media that entertain, such as motion pictures and television programs, may have great emotional impact. These may lend themselves to longer-range and indirect programs of interpretation. Educational materials, books, and pamphlets, which can supply strong factual support, while direct, are also more suitable for longer-range interpretation.

Television has the largest audience. The vivid, attention-seizing character of television news convinces by means of direct visual presentations and contemporaneity. Therefore television news has great power to crystalize opinion or action in response to specific events touching people's lives. However, television is better for quick, colorful presentations than for thoughtful analysis, which requires a longer attention span. The considerable emotional impact of messages embodied in television entertainment programs tends to be less specific. Lack of specificity also characterizes the impact of other emotionally powerful media, such as motion pictures, drama, novels, and cartoons. Without appropriate follow-up these communications may be missed, misinterpreted, have little effect, or evoke an unintended backlash.

Newspapers and journals of comment reach much smaller audiences. However, they are followed closely by opinion leaders and persons in responsible positions. Thus, they may be effective in influencing significant public and private decisions on major issues.

Messages in the specialized media, such as trade papers, the labor press, church journals, and ethnic papers, are concerned primarily with matters of specific interest to the group. Yet messages in these specialized media may be very effective because of their concentrated impact on the group leadership, who can then communicate with the broader membership of the group.

Letters to the editor are widely read. Given appropriate authorship, they, like op-ed articles, may convey positive interpretation. Advertisements may be eye-catching, but they have a serious drawback—they may be dismissed as partisan and therefore not acceptable.

Radio, which can reach people in offices or cars, offers opportunities for concentrated, short communications. These may also reach rural areas otherwise inaccessible. Talk shows, which hold extensive audiences, require special attention; if they are conducted by ill-informed or arbitrary hosts, they may disseminate destructive messages.

Rallies, demonstrations, and various forms of public activity and social action may enhance the impact on attitudes of messages in the media. These can personalize the messages and bring them home to the public and to influentials. By attracting television and press coverage, they may be brought to the attention of a very broad segment of the public. It is better to create news that will have a favorable impact indirectly than to issue self-serving releases.

45. Combating Negative Images

For combating false and unfavorable images in the media, the Jewish community relations field utilizes the constant presentation of positive messages in a simple, direct, straightforward form.[64]

Discussion: This strategic principle is of considerable importance, but it is as difficult in application as the principle regarding the need to adapt the message to the recipient (Number 43). The natural tendency, if anti-Semitic or anti-Israel or generally bigoted material is in circulation through the media, is to shout a response emotionally and emphatically. This is not always the most effective reaction. Any action, of course, assumes that there has been effective monitoring, that the facts are known accurately, checked, and interpreted adequately.

It is frequently impossible to catch up with a lie or a misleading statement. Cool factual analysis, if possible from a source matching or surpassing the prestige and authority of the person making the charge or creating the misinterpretation, is necessary for the record; but efforts to obtain the same prominent display for replies as for sensational allegations are seldom successful. The media usually do not regard responses as equally newsworthy.

The problem in dealing with negative images through the media reflects the preoccupation of each person with his or her own concerns, as noted in earlier strategic principles (see, e.g., Numbers 42 and 43). Correcting misstatements has problems in addition to the difficulty of getting people to attend to anything not touching them directly and to absorb its meaning. Attempts to refute by argument and evidence bore the casual viewer or reader. Exhortation and moralizing repel. Defensive pleading arouses suspicion rather than sympathy. Besides, efforts at direct refutation tend to spread the original canard further, and thus to do more harm than good. The specific lie must never be repeated. This was the "strategy of error" of the German Jews in dealing with the beginnings of the Hitler madness.[65]

For a more promising approach it is necessary to emulate the Confederate general who said that he won battles by getting there first with the most. The effective substitute for refutation is the constant presentation, in appropriate ways, of positive messages. A continuing program of positive interpretation, especially one initiated before the specific problem arose, can blunt and forestall the negative statements.

This strategic principle has been borne out by experience time after time. Giving in to natural impulse and ignoring it, as is sometimes done, is likely to be at best wasteful and possibly harmful.

46. Use of Media within the Community Relations Program

The use of the mass media is one of many interrelated components of the total Jewish community relations program.[66]

Discussion: The glamor of the mass media, the heavy reliance that candidates for political office place on their media images, and the alleged power of the media to mold events (did Walter Cronkite bring Sadat to Jerusalem to negotiate with Begin?) have led to a great emphasis on their use for community relations purposes. When employment of the media is in accordance with the preceding principles, media usage can be valuable. But it is important to keep in mind that every part of the Jewish community relations program is related to every other part, and the success of any specific activity or project depends on the success of the total program. (The answer to the question about Sadat is: "Not bloody likely!")

Image-building and forceful presentation of favorable messages are unlikely to be effective unless embedded in a broader, relevant community relations program. There can be no successful use of the media without the day-by-day, week-by-week process of establishing and maintaining community contacts. Relationships with public officials, Christian clergy, black leaders, academics, editors and publishers, TV producers, and heads of women's organizations, ethnic organizations, and labor unions are necessary to provide the base for media access and coverage. This means maintaining contact with and winning the endorsement of a wide variety of groups, which in turn requires Jewish community relations attention to the issues in which the various groups and individuals have a spontaneous interest.

Without such contacts, efforts to approach the media can be ineffectual, and there may be danger of a backlash. With such contacts, media can be approached successfully, positive materials can be proposed and used, and follow-up action in a variety of ways can achieve successful outcomes.

American Jewry, World Jewry, and Geopolitics

"We are one!" was the slogan of a massive campaign for funds to meet Jewish needs in this country and all over the world. This is of course an expression of an ancient concept, that Jews everywhere are brothers and sisters. All Jews are part of a worldwide Jewish community, bound together by a common history and tradition, by common aims for peace and justice in the world, and by recognition of a common destiny. It is this benevolent feeling of kinship that anti-Semites have so distorted in their destructive myths.

With characteristic gallows humor, Jews have condensed the lessons of centuries of oppression into the saying, "It's hard to be a Jew." It may be difficult for the younger generation of Jews in the United States to know what this bitter apothegm can mean, even though there may have been some rise in the chart of anti-Semitic occurrences in this country in very recent times. But while young Jews may not experience it in their personal lives, they have only to look abroad at the plight of many fellow Jews, and American Jewry is aware of this.

In Israel, still fighting for its existence almost thirty-five years after it became the real embodiment of an age-old dream and commitment, the wondrous achievements and the courage of its citizens are challenged daily. American

Jews regard it as part of their communal life to help Israel in this struggle. The enemies of Israel are attacking Jews all over the world in the name of opposition to a straw-man "Zionism" that bears no resemblance to true Jewish aspirations. Jews in the Soviet Union and in Moslem lands, which are engaged in geopolitical struggles with Israel, are subjected to a variety of oppressive measures, usually under the specious cover of "anti-Zionism." But this contagious lie is not always needed; explicit old-fashioned anti-Semitic oppression exists in some despotisms. In Latin America, for instance, the situation in many countries is dubious at best.

Because the United States is a pluralistic democratic nation, and a great power, the American Jewish community is in a position to speak for threatened Jews in other lands. American Jews are almost unique in their capacity to help endangered Jews, and play a vital role in their preservation.

Some of the earliest community relations efforts of Jews in this free country, dating deep back into the nineteenth century (protesting the Mortara forced conversion, for instance), sought to mobilize American public opinion and obtain aid for oppressed Jews abroad. Two of the most active Jewish community relations agencies today, the American Jewish Committee and the American Jewish Congress, were founded initially to deal with problems of Jews overseas. The specific occasion for the establishment of the American Jewish Committee, in 1906, was to seek an appropriate American response to pogroms in what is now the Soviet Union. The American Jewish Congress was set up following World War I to represent Jewish concerns in the peace-making process. In 1922 it became a formal organization when some of its leaders wanted to maintain a continuing process.

Interpretation and action regarding Israel, Jews in the Soviet Union, Jews in Moslem lands, Falashas, and Jews in Latin America are necessary and important aspects of Jewish community relations programming in the United States today.

The following strategic principles have been developed to guide programming in these areas, supplementing the principles already stated, which of course apply to these concerns as well.

47. Cooperation with Jewish Communities in Foreign Lands

To the extent feasible, American Jewish community relations agencies make statements and take public actions designed to benefit the Jews of another country only after consideration of the situation and opinions of those Jews.[67]

Discussion: This is a fundamental strategic principle, but one that is extremely difficult to apply in practice. What is at stake is the autonomy, to say nothing of the on-the-spot expertise, of Jewish communities abroad, and the autonomy of the American Jewish community as well.

The Jews in this country are American citizens; they have the right, and the obligation, to exercise their own judgment when they call upon the American people or the U.S. government to take action on questions of human rights abroad, including those of Jews in other countries. On the other hand, if the Jews in another country have an uncoerced view about what is good for them, obviously American Jews would not want to ignore and override it without at least giving it earnest consideration.

In such democratic nations as Canada, France, or Great Britain, there is no problem in consulting and cooperating with the Jews. It may still be difficult to apply the principle, because in democratic countries different Jewish groups may be of different opinions. But these are not the countries where the deep dilemmas lie. Jews in democratic countries act along with American Jews to help those who most need assistance.

With regard to the Jews in Israel, close to the focus of the American Jewish community's concerns, there is constant intercommunication. The range of opinions is as wide in democratic Israel as in democratic America. Also, Israel is a national state, and not just a community of Jews; the views of the administration in power do not stand in the same relation to American Jews as the views of, say, the Canadian Jewish Congress for Canada. American Jews, in their constant effort to mobilize support for Israel, must exercise their own judgment, after considering carefully the views expressed in Israel.

At the opposite extreme, little can be determined of the views of Jews in the lands of deepest trouble, such as Ethiopia, Syria, and Iran. It is even difficult to ascertain facts. News and opinions come from recent emigres and escapees, and sometimes messages can find their way indirectly out of the country. But these Jews are not free, and no one can tell which views are representative and which are coerced by fear. American Jews must, after the most careful deliberations, rely on their own judgment almost entirely.

Puzzling ambiguities occur also when there is partial communication. In the Soviet Union and its satellites, there may be communications with individuals, even where internal organization of the Jewish community is prohibited. It is never clear what may have been subtly distorted by pressures and disinformation. In some Latin American countries, such as Argentina, there is an organized Jewish community which does express its views, but it is difficult to determine at a distance whether the Jewish leadership is in fact representative and free to express itself. The controversy about Jacobo Timerman's charges exemplifies these complexities.

This strategic principle is almost as difficult to apply as the ant's advice to the grasshopper to turn himself into a cockroach. Where the communication is best, the problems are least pressing; where the problems are most urgent, communication is likely to be least practical. That is why the statement of the principle contains a reservation on grounds of feasibility. But it is nevertheless a useful and even necessary guide to action in these very complicated areas of programming.

48. Interpretation Regarding Israel

The Jewish community relations field seeks to interpret to the American people, the national administration, the Congress, and influentials generally that Israel deserves support as a friendly, democratic, modern, and humanitarian nation, which serves as a reliable strategic asset to the United States in the Middle East.[68]

Discussion: There is a bewildering paradox: that Israel—democratic, humanitarian, peaceloving, and already accepting painful risks and sacrifices for mutual accommodation with Egypt, as it would with all its neighbors—is all too often characterized as intransigent and expansionist; while the Arab states and groupings, which with the exception of Egypt still adhere to the post–1967 War Khartoum resolution regarding Israel (they say "the Zionist entity")—no negotiations, no recognition, no peace—seem increasingly to be accepted as the peace-seeking parties. The murderous PLO, committed to Israel's destruction, is increasingly believed when it represents the Palestinian Arabs as victims of Israeli brutality and genocide, denied elementary rights of self-determination.

Except for Egypt, what the Arab powers are seeking is peace *without* Israel, rather than peace with Israel. The Camp David Accords alone have advanced peace with justice in the Middle East. They point the way to a resolution of the problems through negotiations without preconditions. These simple facts have been rendered obscure to the American people, for a number of reasons.

Americans regard themselves as fair, kindly, brave, and possessed of other good qualities. By and large, the American people, to the extent that they think about the Middle East at all, are much more likely to attribute these favorable characteristics to Israel than to its enemies. Polls show that, on balance, American public opinion toward Israel is still positive, but not by so wide a margin as before the worldwide propaganda campaign to denigrate Israel was intensified in recent years.

The total image of Israel has been distorted by various charges and misconceptions of militarism, religious fanaticism, racism, imperialism, intransigence, and injustice. Even the themes that are favorable for Israel's image may not be unambiguous. For instance, Israel's strength and military readiness may be regarded positively by veterans' groups and negatively by some antiwar student groups; biblical text as justification may weigh heavily with Christian fundamentalist groups but may be ignored by liberal religionists; vocal democratic dissent in Israel may appeal to some and appear to others as disunity; and so forth.

Most potent of the factors affecting public opinion regarding Israel is the attitude of the national Administration, especially as revealed in public statements and actions of the President. Foreign-policy issues seem remote and abstruse to the public, two-thirds of which admits to virtually no interest in foreign affairs. Statements by the President of the United States tend to be accepted as guides to what is in the national interest; this is true even in periods when a President's popularity may be low. The President commands media attention. Leaks, true or planted, and confidential briefings of journalists, have a potent effect on public opinion, and specifically on elite opinion. The patriotic responses in crises, rallying around the President, reinforce the prestige of the office in guiding public opinion. To a lesser extent, prestige enhances the opinion-molding power of those associated with the President—the Secretary of State, the Secretary of Defense—and of members of Congress and other national influentials.

Thus it is necessary to be able to communicate effectively for interpretation of Israel with the centers of power in the country, not just because they have the authority to make the crucial decisions, but because, at least in the short run, they have more capacity to influence public opinion than public opinion has to influence them. The initiative in the first instance is that of the national leaders, responding to situational analyses and the balance of forces among influentials, with public opinion following.

Two principal goals of the Jewish community relations program of interpretation regarding Israel have been continued United States military and economic support at levels needed to assure Israel the means of self-defense and economic viability; and the avoidance of undue pressure on Israel by the United States in its legitimate efforts to maintain good relationships with other Mideast nations. Good relationships need not require arming Israel's avowed enemies or exacting debilitating concessions from Israel without true peace negotiations. The need for maintaining continued administration and congressional support for Israel is thus imperative. Congress has taken the lead in such support at times, the administration at other times; the Jewish community relations agencies must maintain effective contact with both, at all times.

Other influentials with whom constant communication regarding Israel is required include state and local officials, candidates and political-party functionaries, as well as the media, business and labor leaders, academics, clergy, and other such opinion leaders.

The main themes of the interpretation have been:

- the imperative need for direct negotiations without preconditions between Israel and her Arab neighbors, recognized to date only by Egypt
- the need for defensible "secure and recognized" borders for Israel, in accordance with the key United Nations Security Council Resolution 242
- the need to keep meddling by the U.S.S.R. and the U.N. General Assembly out of future peace negotiations since both are biased and inimical (in this connection it should be noted that the Camp David Accords, formal agreements among Israel, Egypt, and the United States and the only peace treaty involving Israel, were made possible by direct negotiations without the participation of troublemakers)
- the impossibility of recognizing or dealing with the Palestine Liberation Organization, which practices terrorism, is committed to the destruction of Israel, and maintains its dubious claim to represent the Palestinian Arabs in large part by murder and intimidation of other voices
- the historic right of Israel to Jerusalem, as further demonstrated by its scrupulous care in cherishing the holy places of all faiths, with administration of the sites by the faiths themselves.

The struggle for American support has been successful, for the most part. In the face of a massive propaganda assault upon Israel financed by unlimited Arab oil money, reinforced by economic pressure, boycott, and blackmail, and abetted by the political and military machinations of a great power, the Soviet Union, the great preponderance of editorial comment in local newspapers throughout the country has been consistently favorable to Israel—though some nationally syndicated columnists and cartoonists have been less so—and in general successive administrations and congresses have been supportive. Arab boycotts have been checked and countered. There have been numerous expressions of support by officials and by leaders of church bodies, unions, and ethnic and other groups. But this is a battle that can never be won once and for all. Constant effort is necessary.

As the propaganda drive intensifies, pressures against United States support for Israel accumulate from every side. Liberal Protestants and pacifists believe that Israel's self-defense and assertion of its rights to defend its people are militaristic. Japan and European nations, and powerful business interests in this country, think that throwing Israel to the wolves is a small price to pay for continued oil flow, and believe that the Arabs would be genuinely grateful and cooperative if Israel were sacrificed. Ill-conceived plans are launched by various officials to carry water on both shoulders, and appease the Arabs while assuring Israel of friendship.

In a situation of this sort, there is considerable danger that some actors on the national scene may stimulate anti-Israel and, directly or indirectly, anti-Semitic feelings in the effort to carry out the pro-Arab policies that may seem to be blocked by those sensitive to Israel's needs. Virulent anti-Semitism can be set off by people who do not regard themselves as anti-Semites—they feel that they are simply engaged in normal political give-and-take. They either do not realize, or do not care, that they are spreading a dangerous virus which history has proved to be contagious and destructive. When the anti-Semitism is overt, it should be challenged, but all the preceding principles must not be neglected, and the Jewish community should not allow itself to be diverted from the main task—the interpretation of Israel—to sudden anxiety about its own security.

The importance of the valid principle of interpretation of

Israel is therefore evident. If adequate interpretation has been proceeding in accordance with this strategic guideline, there is little danger that Israel will lack friends and under-standing supporters in times of pressure.

49. The Energy Issue

The Jewish community relations field regards the energy situation as a worldwide geopolitical threat with serious domestic reflections, but not as an issue inherent in the Arab-Israel conflict.[69]

Discussion: At the time of the Arab oil embargo in 1973, which the enemies of Isarel attempted to use as a lever for anti-Israel propaganda and pressure, the American people suffered and complained, but they did not fall into the error of blaming Israel. A lesson had already been learned from the Arab attempts, not only to boycott Israel, but also to enforce a secondary boycott against the American firms that maintained normal business relationships with Israel. This was so obviously violative of all democratic principles that it was finally banned by law, insofar as efforts to enforce compliance by United States firms were concerned.

The Arab oil embargo and the continuing squeeze exerted by the huge OPEC oil-price boosts served to alert the world, earlier than might otherwise have been the case, to the fact that a global energy crisis was impending, and thus to stimulate protective action along a number of lines: conser-vation, exploitation of oil and gas resources formerly less feasible economically, development of alternative energy sources—nuclear, coal, solar, wind, water, and renewable biological sources such as wood and alcohol. In the United States, this has led to domestic controversies over such issues as deregulation and windfall-profits taxes. The economic and geopolitical consequences of immense Arab financial power, with dollars drained from the United States through high oil prices and then reinvested through purchase and control of resources here, have had a large, but diffuse, impact on the American political scene.

This valid principle on energy means that the Jewish community relations field has an obligation to familiarize itself with the intricacies of energy economics and politics in this country. This is necessary partly in order to pursue effectively the basic policy of serving the general welfare. Partly, also, it is necessary in order to ensure that energy problems cannot be used, speciously, for anti-Israel and anti-Semitic purposes. Questions concerning energy addressed in the Joint Program Plan for 1981–82 include decontrol, wind-fall-profits tax, alternative-energy development, strategic reserve, and coal resources.

50. The United Nations and Human Rights

In support of peace and worldwide human welfare, the original aims of the United Nations, the Jewish community relations field condemns and exposes the progressive subversion of the U.N. into an instrument of propaganda and political manipulation by a cynical bloc of Soviet, Arab, and Third World nations.[70]

Discussion: The Jewish community strongly supported the idea of the United Nations, and cherished great hopes for it as an instrument for peace and international cooperation.

Security Council Resolutions 242 and 338 have been accepted by Israel and most Arab nations but have never been endorsed by the self-styled Palestine Liberation Organization. These resolutions supplied the foundation for the Camp David agreements, and could still furnish a basis for peace negotiations to settle the Middle East conflict, if there were equity in the U.N. But over the years the U.N. has been tilted heavily against the interests of Israel and of the free world generally. This reflects the voting power of the Arab and Moslem bloc in the U.N. and the success of Soviet propaganda linking Israel and the United States and its friends with hated colonialism. Through economic necessity Israel has had some commercial relations with South Africa, as many black African nations do also. Propaganda efforts have repeatedly attempted to identify Israel with that country's abominable apartheid policies, although both Israel and American Jewish organizations have repeatedly denounced apartheid.[71]

The most deplorable sign of the deterioration of the U.N. was the adoption by the General Assembly, where there is no veto, of a vicious propagandistic resolution condemning Zionism as racism. This has since been used repeatedly by the Soviets and the Arabs (in at least one of whose states slavery still exists), not only to discredit Israel, but to spread anti-Semitism throughout the world under the cover of opposing "racist Zionism." This canard has damaged the formerly close cooperative relationship of some American blacks with American Jews, as well as their image of Israel. With this tool, low-road propaganda has attempted to undermine the influence and good name of the United States by charging that this country is dominated by "Zionist imperialists."

The Jewish community relations agencies have urged continued support of the purposes for which the U.N. was established and continued U.S. membership. They have called upon U.S. representatives to take full advantage of various U.N. forums to uphold democratic freedoms and to expose and denounce the misuse and subversion of those forums. Also, they have pressed the U.N. Secretariat for rigorous adherence to merit in appointing, assigning, and promoting U.N. personnel, rather than bowing to political pressures. Because the deterioration has progressed so far, the Jewish community relations agencies have advocated the withholding of portions of U.S. payments to the U.N. and selectively to its specialized agencies, in proportion to the seriousness of the injuries to international relations posed by particular circumstances.

Outside the structure of the U.N., a very large-scale effort toward establishment and implementation of human rights internationally was made at the Helsinki Conference in 1975. In exchange for recognition of Soviet-established boundary lines in Europe, the Soviet Union accepted a "third basket" guaranteeing rights to individuals within their countries. The U.S.S.R. and its satellites, however, have blocked the implementation of these commitments, steadfastly distorting their intent and misrepresenting facts at follow-up conferences in Belgrade and Madrid. Jewish organizations have supported the efforts of successive U.S. representatives to press for realization of the promised human rights.

This valid and important principle demonstrates the close interrelationship of programs for Jewish community relations and for human rights, in this country and throughout the world.

51. Jews in the Soviet Union

The Jewish community relations field seeks a liberalization of the U.S.S.R.'s emigration policies for Jews in the Soviet Union, and the right of Jews who continue to live in the Soviet Union to do so freely as Jews.[72]

Discussion: There was virtually no Jewish emigration from the Soviet Union prior to 1965. Since then, over a quarter of a million Jews have left, despite fluctuations in Soviet regulations and severe harassment of Jews applying for visas. This has included arbitrary delays, harsh and exploitative regulations, unexplained rejections, firing from jobs, splitting of families, and severe jail sentences of some applicants on trumped-up charges.

Such relaxation as has occurred cannot easily be traced to specific causes. Unquestionably, however, vigorous public agitation by the Jews of America and elsewhere has sensitized the world to the plight of Soviet Jewry, and, in fact, of all repressed dissidents. This has had a double effect. It has strengthened the morale of the Jews in the Soviet Union and has given them the courage to resist, which in turn has inspired Jews everywhere. And it has mobilized actions by the United States which the Soviets could not ignore.

Action by the United States government has been an essential factor in the struggle for freer emigration. A powerful lever on Soviet practices has been the Jackson-Vanik Amendment, which provides that United States credit and trade concessions to the Soviet Union be commensurate with the degree of fairness of the emigration policies and practices of the U.S.S.R. This law requires that the President before waiving trade restrictions find that there has been fairness.

Nevertheless, the Soviet Union has incited anti-Semitism among its people, who have been highly susceptible to this virus for centuries. The U.S.S.R. has rigorously limited

Jewish employment in professional and technical occupations, and has shut off or restricted Jewish access to higher and technical education. The deliverance of Jews from the repression that confronts them and their children in the Soviet Union is therefore all the more urgent.

Jewish community relations agencies have sought to: (1) sustain the morale of Soviet Jews and their determination to find means to reinforce their identity and to continue to apply for permission to emigrate; (2) maintain high American awareness of the plight of Soviet Jews and public opinion condemnatory of the U.S.S.R.'s emigration policy; and (3) assure continued efforts in diplomatic and trade discussions by our government to obtain Soviet liberalization of Jewish emigration.

The programs and activities developed by national and local Jewish community relations agencies, with analysis and information from the National Conference on Soviet Jewry and consultation through the NJCRAC, have been varied and extensive. They have included demonstrations, public meetings, parades and other massed shows of concern, picketing of Soviet trade shows and performances by Soviet artists, organization of committees of specialists such as lawyers or engineers, involvement of public figures in Project Yachad (i.e., correspondence with Jewish families in the U.S.S.R.), stimulation of legislative resolutions and executive proclamations, organization of activities around Jewish holidays and significant anniversary dates, placement of books and furnishing of teaching aids for schools, and many others. Such activities have obtained news coverage or comment in the mass media. The involvement of organizations, corporate enterprise, churches, and others, has also spread public awareness of the issues.

One tactic sometimes proposed, boycott of the Soviet Union, is in general beyond the resources of the Jewish community. In the period of the Hitler menace it was possible to organize a massive and successful anti-Nazi boycott, but this was at a time when most Americans were becoming aware of the danger. Trade relationships were simpler in those days. Even the efforts of the United States government to boycott the Moscow Olympic Games and to embargo grain sales were less than fully successful. Boycott does not appear to be an advisable program instrumentality.

Violent action against the embassies or officials of the Soviet Union, or of any other country, is also counterproductive, and is not advocated or practiced by Jewish community relations agencies.

52. Jews in Troubled Lands

The Jewish community relations field seeks basic human rights for Jews in lands of trouble and oppression in whatever ways that are feasible and appropriate to the situation.[73]

Discussion: An estimated 20,000 or more Jews live in Ethiopia under conditions of poverty, disease, hunger, and ever-present danger. Iran's Jewish community of perhaps 35,000 live in constant fear. In Syria, Jewish emigration is banned, and Jews, as always, have frequently been the victims of spreading disorder and violent factional strife. Jews in other Moslem lands are subjected to similar conditions, in varying degrees. Throughout Latin America, the security of Jewish communities has been threatened by right-left political struggles, and the problems have been accentuated by incessant PLO anti-Zionist, anti-Israel, and anti-Jewish propaganda. Violations of human rights are flagrant and widespread in many countries. Jews are among the thousands of Argentinians who have been imprisoned or have disappeared—because of their alleged political views. Many of the Jewish prisoners have been subjected to especially harsh treatment by interrogators and guards. This occurs in the South American country with the largest Jewish population; similar outrages have been reported in Chile, Uruguay, and other Latin American countries.

In some countries, as in Latin America, U.S. officials may be in a position to intercede in appropriate cases. However, in many of the lands of oppression there is hostility to the United States, and few formal avenues for pressure. Constant alertness and monitoring are needed in all situations; beyond that, specific programs can be devised only with the most careful deliberation and after consultation with those best informed. Where there are emigres or escapees in lands of freedom, as there are Falashas (Ethiopian Jews) in Israel, contact must be maintained with them.

53. Humane Immigration

The Jewish community relations field supports fair and humane American policies with regard to immigration and treatment of newcomers, affecting both Jews and non-Jews.[74]

Discussion: Members of the American Jewish community are descendants of immigrants who benefited from the open immigration policies of this country in the past. They opposed the restrictive McCarran-Walter Act, not solely on behalf of Jews, but as a humanitarian action. This bad legislation in 1952 continued and worsened a 1924 law which rested on the odious principle of quotas and the assumption that some types of immigrants were inherently better than others. Its provisions have since been mitigated.

At the present time there are several million persons living and working in the United States who entered without complying with American immigration law. Most of these "illegal aliens" or "undocumented persons" came here out of desperation in search of opportunities for work and livelihood. In some instances this peaceful invasion has been accepted, on the basis of American humanitarianism. Large numbers of people escaping from intolerable conditions in their lands of origin have been afforded official status—such as the boat people of Indochina, the Cubans, and some Haitians. Various forms of legislation, some generous and some questionable, have been proposed to deal with the undocumented-alien situation. The Jewish community relations agencies have insisted that the undocumented aliens should be accorded basic human services—health care, free public education, assurance of due process, minimum wages, and other fair treatment.

As long ago as 1952, in the struggle against the McCarran-Walter Act, the Jewish community relations agencies advocated immigration and naturalization policies for the United States that

1. establish equitable criteria for admission free from any form of racial, religious, ethnic, or national discrimination
2. allow immigration flexibly adjusted from time to time to the maximum extent compatible with the absorptive capacity of our nation
3. make special provisions for admitting immigrants who seek to become reunited with family members already resident in this country, displaced persons, and refugees, and at the same time safeguard against the admission of those who have themselves participated in persecution of others
4. apply laws equally to naturalized and native-born citizens
5. recognize no basis for deportation of lawfully admitted immigrants other than false or fraudulent representations on application for entry
6. accord immigrants, would-be immigrants, and resident aliens fair hearings, rights of appeal, and other judicial protections against misused or abused administrative authority in regard to exclusion, naturalization, or deportation.

A most painful dilemma regarding immigration rights and the traditional welcome that Jews who are established in this country have always given to new Jewish arrivals has arisen in connection with immigration of Jews who have managed to leave the Soviet Union. The sadistic Soviet regime, seeking ways to multiply the difficulties of emigration for Jews, has issued visas only for Israel, which wants and needs the Soviet Jews. But on reaching free soil (they must exit via Austria), a large proportion of the Jews have instead opted to go to this country, or to Canada or Australia or New Zealand, where they anticipate better economic prospects. It has been suggested that these people have been confused by the stream of anti-Zionist propaganda to which they have been subjected all their lives, and that more of them might choose Israel as a place of resettlement if the American Jewish community were less eager to extend to them the inducements of generous immigration assistance. Furthermore, the Soviets have used the low proportion of emigres actually going to Israel as a pretext for further restrictions. More analysis and consideration of the specifics of this thorny issue will be required.

It can hardly be expected that American Jews, the children of immigrants, will fail to recognize the validity of the principle of humane immigration, as applied to Jews or non-Jews.

54. Remembering the Holocaust

The Jewish community keeps alive the memory of the Holocaust, not only as an indelible part of Jewish history, but as a symbol and warning that human beings are capable of genocide.[75]

Discussion: In this country and throughout the world, there is a whole body of writings being spawned and circulated for the express purpose of denigrating, and even denying, the Holocaust and its meaning. In part this is a special form of paranoid anti-Semitic drivel, in part a contorted effort to assuage German war guilt, and in part a calculated effort to negate the natural sympathy for Israel as a nation of death-camp survivors.

In addition to the Six Million, five million of the victims of the Nazi crematoria and death camps were not Jews, but Poles, Gypsies, homosexuals, communists, etc. They were destroyed because they were "non-Aryan" or were adjudged economically unproductive, "eugenically unfit," or simply politically hostile. The diabolical machinery of Nazism that claimed their lives was the same machinery that took six million Jewish lives. Those who planned the atrocities are equally guilty of the same heinous crimes against humanity, whoever their victims. Those who failed to protest and oppose those crimes must bear the same burden of shame and remorse.

It is not to deny or diminish any of this, or to withhold pity for any of Hitler's victims, to say that the Holocaust was, nonetheless, uniquely a Jewish tragedy. The Nazis' "final solution" envisioned nothing less than the elimination of the Jews as an entire people and of every vestige of Jewish faith, culture, and tradition. It was a savage transformation of a civilized nation into a raging horde following a hate-maddened demagogue. The world must understand: that self-destructive madness had its roots in anti-Semitism, against which guard must ever be maintained in the name of sanity. For that reason the Holocaust must be perceived as a Jewish experience: not for the sake of Jews, but for the sake of a world which must never suffer a rebirth of Nazism.

There has been an encouraging increase in study and interpretation of the Holocaust, including television and theatrical productions, books and articles, teaching about the Holocaust in schools and universities, organized visits to the sites of Nazi death camps and to Yad Vashem, and observances of Days of Remembrance. An official U.S. Holocaust Memorial Council has been formed and has been active, drawing some criticism from crypto-bigots.

The greater understanding, however, has not resulted in Senate ratification of the U.N. Convention against Genocide, which years ago was .blocked by the solid opposition of anti–civil rights senators.

The NJCRAC Joint Program Plan for 1981–82 notes among other specific applications of the strategic principle of remembering the Holocaust:

- development and dissemination of teaching and study materials, for use in public and parochial junior and senior high schools, colleges, and universities
- seminars for educators; conferences with church leaders
- placement of printed and audiovisual materials in school libraries
- joint commemorative activities with Holocaust survivors
- oral history projects; creation of memorials, such as permanent exhibits, monuments, plaques, and special library shelves
- visits to Yad Vashem in Israel, and tours of European ghetto and camp sites
- cooperation with "Pages of Testimony," Yad Vashem's documentation projects of names, vital statistics, and circumstances of death of victims

- annual observances in the spring of Holocaust Heroes and Martyrs Day in states and localities and, nationally, of the Days of Remembrance of Victims of the Holocaust.

55. Prosecution of Alleged Nazi War Criminals

The Jewish community relations field advocates and supports vigorous prosecution of former Nazis.[76]

Discussion: There is reason to believe that, after long complacency and unconcern, the U.S. government has begun to ferret out and prosecute Nazi war criminals who for years have lived in this country unmolested. An Office of Special Investigations has been formed in the Justice Department.

In the period of confusion following World War II, many Nazi camp guards or collaborators, especially natives of countries invaded by Hitler, managed to migrate to the United States, entering without revealing their past records. It is estimated that there are 250 Nazi criminals living in the United States.

The thirty- to thirty-five-year lag in prosecution of former Nazis who concealed their records from immigration authorities has greatly complicated the preparation of cases and the location of surviving witnesses. Recently Poland and the U.S.S.R., where many witnesses live, have facilitated the taking of depositions and in some cases the videotaping of statements for court presentation.

A special problem is the fact that some of the former Nazis have become members in this country of ethnic associations which reject the allegations against them. There is some danger of fanning sparks of anti-Semitism among ethnic, neighborhood, or religious groups with which the war criminals (not known as such) have become identified. These strains can be alleviated by programs for good intergroup relations.

In accordance with this principle, Jewish community relations agencies should continue to monitor the progress of the cases against the former Nazis as they are identified.

PROCEDURAL
PRINCIPLES

Substantive questions of Jewish community relations can never be settled once and for all. No answer has ever been complete or perfect. This is true at the level of strategy and policy as well as that of tactics in specific situations. Therefore old answers can never be applied mechanically without fresh consideration. The policies and strategic principles can supply the foundation for each new assessment, but only within a continuing process of planning.

Planning involves bringing together representatives of the different voices in the community and resources in the Jewish community relations field. All the various analyses and expectations are matched up. Alternative scenarios regarding different actions are followed out. Then agreement can be reached on a program (usually a complex one with multiple roles and approaches, because problems are seldom simple) and upon the ways that the existing resources can be deployed to accomplish the agreed ends. Of course such planning is never finished. There must be continuous review, updating, modification, adaptation. It is in actuality this planning process that maintains the continuity of Jewish community relations through shifting situations and changing priorities.

The substantive policy statements and strategic principles

therefore require supplementation by a set of formal or procedural principles, to serve as guides in the planning process. Such procedural principles are as important as the substantive principles.

56. Common Cause

All the Jewish community relations agencies seek to serve the interests, not only of their constituencies, but of the entire Jewish community.[77]

Discussion: The first and most important procedural principle is that Jews recognize a common cause, and hence a basis for common action in the Jewish interest.

It is of course true that there is no single "Jewish community interest" in the sense of goals receiving the endorsement of every single person in the community. Common cause implies no uniformity. There are significant disagreements. But experience over the past forty years has demonstrated that consensus, rather than conflict, has characterized debates on a great variety of issues. Differences within the Jewish community field have been fewer and less serious than might have been expected.

This principle means that, regardless of legitimate differences about what constitutes the Jewish community interest, all Jewish community relations programs are designed to serve what each agency conceives as the common cause rather than any partisan objective within the community.

57. Community Organization

Effective planning and conduct of the Jewish community relations program rests on organization of the Jewish community.[78]

Discussion: This principle means that no single individual or organization, however powerful or brilliant or widely known, can assume without consultation the role of spokesperson for the Jewish community and for the Jews of America. Through a process of community organization, truly representative spokespersons can voice truly representative views in the names of those who endorse them.

Community organization is a continuing process rather

than a condition or an end-state. The goal is united action to meet common community problems through machinery for joint consultation, exchange of views, effort to reach agreement on action, and provision of resources in readiness to implement decisions.

A variety of agencies with specialized responsibilities have been created to serve Jewish communal needs and purposes. Besides community relations agencies, these include:

- agencies concerned with services to individuals, such as Jewish hospitals, family services, services to the aged, child-care agencies, vocational services, and migration services
- agencies concerned with services to groups and with the furtherance of Jewish life, including Jewish community centers, Jewish educational programs, and cultural institutions
- agencies concerned with community planning and fund-raising, such as federations and national organizations for planning and fund-raising.

These agencies constitute the structure of the organized Jewish community.

From time to time the question is raised: "How truly democratic are the processes of Jewish community organization?" This of course depends on the concept of democracy that is appropriate. If the sole criterion is "One man (person!), one vote!" the process and structure could be regarded as not genuinely democratic. The procedures of representation are indeed indirect. A member of the Jewish community becomes active in one or more of the kinds of services named, either by making a financial contribution or by volunteering time and effort, or more often both; this entitles him or her to a voice in the naming of a board of directors, which in turn names its officers. These generally name the people who participate in interagency and national planning. This indirect representation is fundamentally democratic, in the sense that it reflects the opinions prevalent among those who participate voluntarily, and participation is open to all who wish to take part. It is doubtful that town-meeting democracy, or any process of voting on issues by all members of the Jewish community, would achieve a more truly representative outcome.

58. Voluntarism

Within the pluralistic structure of the organized Jewish community, agencies and organizations are autonomous and cooperate voluntarily.[79]

Discussion This procedural principle reflects the fact that there is no central authority within Jewish life in America, nor is any needed to coerce joint action. Agencies and organizations cooperate voluntarily, and this form of joint action is not only more appropriate for a free society, but it also has much greater sticking power than would any pseudo-cooperation imposed by external force.

The principle of democratic pluralism applies within the Jewish community as well as in American society generally. There are many subgroups within American Jewry, differing in denomination, observance, country of family origin and generation in this country, cultural background, and approaches to matters of Jewish concern. Many organizations in Jewish life have constituencies drawn in large part from one or another of these distinctive subgroups. This dynamic internal diversity is essential for the vitality of the American Jewish community.

Voluntarism is inherent in pluralism (Number 2). It is reciprocal to and complements the principle of common cause (Number 56). Within the Jewish community, groups and organizations have the same rights of expression and dissent as the Jewish community and all other comparable groups have within the American mosaic. Voluntarism and pluralism, unity and diversity, are the basic and balanced supports of Jewish community organization.

59. Total Community Structure

Every organization identified as Jewish, whatever its function, has an impact on Jewish community relations and plays a role.[80]

Discussion It would be narrow and misleading to think of the agencies that work specifically in the field of Jewish community relations as the only resource for the promotion of good relationships between Jews and non-Jews. All other resources, agencies, and organizations of the Jewish community have natural contacts with American society generally and specifically with their peer groups. Their employment policies and personnel practices impinge on equality of opportunity. They may have policies and practices in regard to such church-state matters as child adoption across religious lines or use of public funds, which affect questions of religious liberty. What they do regarding academic freedom, or the making available of public forums to speakers of various viewpoints, has a bearing on freedom of opinion. Their relationships with other agencies and with individuals are aspects of the quality of Jewish–non-Jewish relationships generally.

Social-welfare and community-service programs are inherently helpful. They minimize individual and social tensions, provide constructive recreational outlets, strengthen neighborhoods and ameliorate slum conditions, promote self-examination of irrational attitudes, afford opportunities for equal-status intergroup contacts in informal situations, and help develop natural leaders. These all significantly foster good community relationships.

The policies and programs of all the Jewish communal services are properly determined by themselves with primary regard to their essential functional responsibilities. Community relations considerations enter as a secondary and supportive aspect of decision-making in the other communal services. Unfortunately, the agencies sometimes lack orientation. Their community relations effectiveness can be enhanced by cooperation with the community relations agencies.

In accordance with this principle, there should be an interpenetration of Jewish community relations concepts and of the concepts that inform the various other communal services. To this end, continuous interconsultation and cooperation are necessary.

60. Involvement

Jewish community relations planning requires involvement of all significant voices in the Jewish community.[81]

Discussion: This procedural principle is an extension of the principle of community organization. Of course there is no feasible way for everybody to be involved directly. Through the representative structures of the organized Jewish community, however, it is possible to open the door to very wide indirect participation, and this is essential. Not every issue is of such importance or delicacy as to require full-scale community debate and formal action. The important consideration is that every Jewish person active in community relations should feel that he or she had an opportunity to adduce views, through whatever structure may be chosen as the avenue of expression.

There are two advantages to wide involvement of the Jewish community. One is the very practical matter of improving the quality of deliberations by inclusion of all informed views, since, as Lincoln pointed out, "everybody is smarter than anybody." The other is the need for imparting a vital element of sanction to programs. If a group or organization has participated in a planning process, even though it may have dissented from the form of action adopted, it is less likely to challenge the legitimacy of the decision. Even the ablest people can make mistakes or can be defeated, at times. The true test of action in the common cause of the entire Jewish community is not just success or failure, but whether at the stage of initiation it had the general sanction of diverse elements in the community. Obviously, community sanction is also needed for funding.

61. Cooperation and Coordination

Jewish community relations agencies participate in a process by which the knowledge, experience, and opinions of all are pooled for the common good.[82]

Discussion: Locally, this essential principle is mediated by the Jewish community relations council that covers the area. Nationally, there is one unique voluntary advisory agency for continuing cooperation and coordination in the Jewish community relations field, the National Jewish Community Relations Advisory Council.

All the member agencies agree to join together in the common cause in cooperative efforts through the NJCRAC to reach agreement on:

1. the issues on which the agencies should take positions
2. what those positions should be
3. the strategies, approaches, and programs best calculated to advance those positions
4. the best means for improving the methods, approaches, and techniques being pursued by the field as a whole
5. the most effective ways of utilizing all the resources available to the field for advancement of joint purposes.

As a result of the cooperative process of sharing information and experience, exchange of views, and determination of consensus, certain judgments, conclusions, and recommendations may be reached jointly. It is understood that these are advisory, and that each agency may adopt, modify, or reject them in accordance with its own best judgment.

To be effective, a cooperative relationship must rest upon:

1. full and complete exchange of knowledge, views, etc., among all the participating agencies
2. true and considerate regard by all for the opinions of each, whether in accord or in disagreement
3. equally true and considerate regard by all for joint judgments and recommendations reached by consensus.

Thus, the NJCRAC is not a separate community relations agency, but a mechanism, a process, through which the agencies seek to agree on:

• Joint Policy Formulation
    What issues to take positions on
    What those positions should be

- Joint Program Planning and Coordination
    What the major problems are
    What should be done to deal with them
    What priority each program should be given
    How the total resources of all the agencies can best be used to advance the entire effort
- Reassessment and Evaluation
    How new developments and findings of social science affect the basic assumptions on which community relations work rests
    How well the methods in use are working
    What better methods might be tried
- Community Consultation
    Focusing all the resources of the field on helping communities to:
    Organize local community relations structures
    Develop local programs
    Orient and train new workers
    Develop their own joint policies and recommendations
    Utilize effectively the resources and functional services of all national agencies
- Information Services
    Continually exchanging information among the cooperating agencies and channeling information and interpretation about the NJCRAC process and its outcomes to the Jewish community
- Personnel Service
    Maintaining information about available openings in the field and helping national and local agencies find qualified personnel; counseling and advising individuals who consider entering the field.

Through the NJCRAC process:

- Jewish community relations policies are formulated with the participation of all agencies and the communities. Differences are argued out in this forum—not publicly. Differences that cannot be reconciled because they rest on fundamental philosophical or ideological disagreements are reduced to basics and clarified, enabling the entire Jewish community to understand them.

- All agencies and communities participate in evaluating new developments and planning how to meet them most effectively so as to advance the jointly adopted policies.
- All agencies and communities are kept informed of what is being done in the field, through an ongoing exchange of information.
- The work of all agencies and communities is coordinated, so that the maximum impact can be had at any given time on crucial issues.
- When there is agreement among the member agencies, a single statement, presentation, congressional testimony, or legal brief may be submitted for all, thus obviating duplicative efforts.
- The affiliated agencies join in continually checking and rechecking the methods and techniques being used and in refining and improving them.

62. National-Local Relationships

National and local Jewish community relations agencies play complementary roles in the general community relations program.[83]

Discussion: The essential point is that national agency actions affect every community, and that local agency actions may have important national consequences. Therefore, in implementation of principle Number 61 on cooperation and coordination, a further specification of procedures for national-local relationships is necessary.

The following statement of principles, adopted by the NCRAC Executive Committee on April 15, 1953, continues to govern national-local relationships:

Jewish community relations agencies are concerned with protecting the rights and furthering the welfare of the Jewish community as a whole and not merely with service to their own members. For this reason, Jewish community relations agencies, national and local, recognize their accountability to the Jewish community in whose cause they serve.

National and local community relations agencies play complementary roles in the general community relations program. Full cooperation and harmony between national and local agencies is imperative for the most effective conduct of community relations activities. Where the local community relations council is representative of the community and involves the participation of the responsible organized groups in the local community or region, its primacy as the central body for local Jewish community relations is recognized.

With respect to their activities and those of their local affiliates as well as in the establishment and operation of branch offices, it should be the policy of national agencies to:

1. Recognize the CRC as the central body with primary responsibility for planning and conducting community relations programs.
2. Encourage their constituents to conduct activities with the approval of the CRC.
3. Place their facilities and resources at the service of the CRC.
4. Encourage the formation of CRCs where they do not now exist.

It should be the policy of CRCs to:

1. Give full recognition to the constituents of national agencies as channels through which the implementation of local community relations programs can be facilitated.
2. Avail themselves of the services of the national agencies.
3. Assist and further the program of local chapters and branches of national agencies.
4. Recognize that no national agency need or should be asked to compromise its fundamental philosophy.

The resolution on national-local relations unanimously adopted on December 16, 1944, is hereby affirmed: If difficulties arise between any national agency and local organization, with respect to the application of the foregoing principles, such difficulties shall be submitted to the N[J]CRAC for its advisory opinion.

SUMMING UP

Recapitulation

The foregoing pages constitute a highly condensed outline of the Jewish community relations field. In one further effort to simplify and cut to the essentials, here is a recapitulation of the main concepts:

Policies

1. The general welfare. The Jewish community relations field seeks to advance the general welfare and to strengthen American democracy, regarding these as the basic guarantees of Jewish security.

2. Democratic pluralism. The Jewish community relations field fosters democratic pluralism, believing that the source of the greatness of the United States and its hospitality to Jews is its success in bringing together people of many origins, religions, and groups on the basis of equality.

3. Majority and minority. The Jewish community relations field does not recognize any group in this country as a majority, entitled to set the norm of Americanism, nor does it regard the Jews (or any other group) as a minority which is part of the American scene only on sufferance and at the price of conformity.

4. Group identity and expression. The Jewish community, like other groups in this country, maintains its own cultural and religious distinctiveness while participating fully through group and individual expression in general American life and affairs.

5. The American Creed. The Jewish community relations field honors and relies upon the American Creed, the ideal of equal rights derived from the Bible, as embodied in the Declaration of Independence and institutionalized in the Constitution and Bill of Rights and in the laws and regulations of the federal government and the several states.

6. The American way. The Jewish community relations field advances the national interest of the United States when it seeks to eliminate imperfections in the implementation of the American Creed.

7. Interdependence. When one group in American society, such as the Jews, acts to uphold the American Creed, it advances the interests of all groups in the country whose rights have been impaired or endangered.

8. Coalition. For the Jewish community, or any other group, to pursue its interests effectively in the public arena, common effort with others is essential.

Strategic Principles
Jewish Security in a Free Society

9. Status of anti-Semitism. Despite fluctuations in overt anti-Semitic manifestations from year to year, the Jewish community relations field does not regard the level of anti-Semitism in the United States as a serious threat at this time.

10. Latent anti-Semitism. The Jewish community relations field regards subsurface anti-Semitism as persistent and potentially threatening.

11. Danger signals. While combating such overt forms of anti-Semitism as violence, vandalism, and defamation, the Jewish community relations field maintains a constant watch for potentially dangerous organized and political forms of anti-Semitism.

12. A menace to Jewish security. Even without explicit anti-Semitism, the Jewish community relations field recognizes a deep menace to Jewish security arising from malfunctions and crises in our society that could threaten American democratic life.

13. Civil liberties. The Jewish community relations field regards the rights of freedom of expression, association, and assembly as essential to the security of Jews, as of all Americans, and therefore seeks to protect the civil liberties of all.

14. Combating anti-Semitism. Since anti-Semitic acts and expressions are widely recognized to be dangers to all Americans rather than to Jews alone, the Jewish community relations field seeks and expects the cooperation of general community resources in combating anti-Semitism.

15. Cults and conversionary movements. The Jewish community relations field resists and regards as harmful the denigration of Judaism and Jewishness by cults and conversionary movements.

16. Rejection of violence. The Jewish community relations field deplores, condemns, and rejects all extralegal forms of violence by or on behalf of Jews against anti-Semites or presumed enemies of Jews.

17. Program for Jewish security. The fundamental strategy of the Jewish community relations field to preserve Jewish security is that of alliance with the self-corrective forces in American society, for the elimination of injustice and poverty, and for the protection of freedom, constitutional rights, and democratic processes.

Social and Economic Justice

18. Unfinished tasks. The Jewish community relations field recognizes the continuing imperfections in American life as threats to the social stability of our democratic nation.

19. Political, economic, and social democracy. The Jewish community relations field regards political, economic, and social justice as interdependent and inseparable aspects of American freedom.

20. Social action. The Jewish community relations field engages in public action to expand opportunities and resources for all, regarding such action as essential to its efforts for the preservation of democratic processes.

21. Government responsibility. The Jewish community relations field, along with voluntary organizations representing other groups in the American mosaic, looks to and calls upon government at all levels to assume responsibilities as appropriate for the implementation of equal rights and opportunities.

22. Women's rights. Consonant with the promotion of equal opportunity and rights for all, the Jewish community relations field supports equal rights for women and prohibition of arbitrary and unreasonable discrimination based on sex.

23. Affirmative action. The Jewish community relations field believes that a just society has an obligation to seek to overcome the evils of past discrimination by affording special help to its victims and hastening their productive participation in the society.

24. Merit. The Jewish community relations field regards merit as the touchstone of equality of opportunity.

25. Balanced program. The Jewish community relations field seeks the improvement of community relationships through a balanced program of social action and education.

Religious Freedom and Church-State Relationships

26. State and religion. The Jewish community relations field believes that democracy in the United States is in large measure a product of the unique principle in our basic law that keeps religion outside the jurisdiction of the state.

27. The public schools and religion. The Jewish community relations field regards the maintenance and furtherance of religion as responsibilities of the synagogue, the church, and the home, and not of the public school system.

28. Sensitive issues. Because of the unusual sensitivity of issues concerning religion and the schools, the Jewish community relations field emphasizes the need for care in planning action, since unwise and poorly timed measures may intensify community relations problems without producing any positive results.

29. Religion and public policy. The Jewish community relations field holds it to be an impairment of religious liberty if any person is penalized for adhering to his or her religious beliefs, or not adhering to any religious belief, so long as he or she does not interfere with the rights of others or endanger the public peace or security.

Interreligious and Intergroup Relationships

30. Mutual respect. The Jewish community relations field seeks to foster intergroup understanding by creating a climate in which groups, and individuals identified with their groups, can develop their fullest potentials in their distinctive ways, rather than by having to deny or minimize group differences.

31. Intergroup conflicts. The Jewish community relations field seeks ways for all groups to live together harmoniously, despite the existence of intergroup differences on doctrines or public issues.

32. Prejudice and stereotypes. The Jewish community relations field combats intergroup tension and hostility by seeking to deal with attitudes, prejudices, and stereotypes.

33. Dispelling misinformation. Imparting correct information is an instrumentality of the Jewish community relations field for combating stereotypes and prejudice.

34. Equal-status contacts. The Jewish community relations field fosters good intergroup relations by bringing people from different groups together in natural equal-status contacts.

35. The law and the reduction of prejudice. The Jewish community relations field looks to the law, as the embodiment of the society's standards, to advance equality not only by its coercive powers, but also through moral force going beyond its sanctions.

36. Common action. The Jewish community relations field believes cooperation of groups for common goals to be especially effective in reducing hostility and prejudice.

Education and the Schools

37. Centrality of the public schools. The Jewish community relations field regards the public schools as the cornerstone of the American democratic system, deserving the full support of the American people.

38. The schools and equality. The Jewish community relations field sees quality integrated education and equal educational opportunities as top-priority goals of American education.

39. Intergroup education. The Jewish community relations field fosters efforts by schools, public and private, to increase intergroup contacts and understanding among children.

40. Financing the public schools. While recognizing that the deficiencies of many public schools are real and by no means exclusively financial, the Jewish community relations field regards adequate financing of the public schools as imperative.

The Mass Media of Communication

41. Goals of mass communication. The Jewish community relations field employs the mass media for concrete, specific goals rather than for general promotion of goodwill or other unspecific aims.

42. Targeting. The Jewish community relations field addresses communications to specific target audiences, each in terms of its own identifications, wants, and needs.

43. Content of communication. The Jewish community relations agencies address the interests and beliefs that the members of the target audience already recognize and hold, rather than attempting to alter their basic concepts.

44. Differential impact of media. In utilizing the various media, the Jewish community relations field takes into consideration their differences in audience and reception.

45. Combating negative images. For combating false and unfavorable images in the media, the Jewish community relations field utilizes the constant presentation of positive messages in a simple, direct, straightforward form.

46. Use of media within the community relations program. The use of the mass media is one of many interrelated components of the total Jewish community relations program.

American Jewry, World Jewry, and Geopolitics

47. Cooperation with Jewish communities in foreign lands. To the extent feasible, American Jewish community relations agencies make statements and take public actions designed to benefit the Jews of another country only after consideration of the situation and opinions of those Jews.

48. Interpretation regarding Israel. The Jewish community relations field seeks to interpret to the American people, the national administration, the Congress, and influentials generally that Israel deserves support as a friendly, democratic, modern, and humanitarian nation, which serves as a reliable strategic asset to the United States in the Middle East.

49. The energy issue. The Jewish community relations field regards the energy situation as a worldwide geopolitical threat with serious domestic reflections, but not as an issue inherent in the Arab-Israel conflict.

50. The United Nations and human rights. In support of peace and worldwide human welfare, the original aims of the United Nations, the Jewish community relations field condemns and exposes the progressive subversion of the U.N. into an instrument of propaganda and political manipulation by a cynical bloc of Soviet, Arab, and Third World nations.

51. Jews in the Soviet Union. The Jewish community relations field seeks a liberalization of the U.S.S.R.'s emigration policies for Jews in the Soviet Union, and the right of Jews who continue to live in the Soviet Union to do so freely as Jews.

52. Jews in troubled lands. The Jewish community relations field seeks basic human rights for Jews in lands of turbulence and oppression in whatever ways that are feasible and appropriate to the situation.

53. Humane immigration. The Jewish community relations field supports fair and humane American policies with regard to immigration and treatment of newcomers, affecting both Jews and non-Jews.

54. Remembering the Holocaust. The Jewish community keeps alive the memory of the Holocaust, not only as an indelible part of Jewish history, but as a symbol and warning that human beings are capable of genocide.

55. Prosecution of alleged Nazi war criminals. The Jewish community relations field advocates and supports vigorous prosecution of former Nazis.

Procedural Principles

56. Common cause. All the Jewish community relations agencies seek to serve the interests, not only of their constituencies, but of the entire Jewish community.

57. Community organization. Effective planning and conduct of the Jewish community relations program rests on organization of the Jewish community.

58. Voluntarism. Within the pluralistic structure of the organized Jewish community, agencies and organizations are autonomous and cooperate voluntarily.

59. Total community structure. Every organization identified as Jewish, whatever its function, has an impact on Jewish community relations and plays a role.

60. Involvement. Jewish community relations planning requires involvement of all significant voices in the Jewish community.

61. Cooperation and coordination. Jewish community relations agencies participate in a process by which the knowledge, experience, and opinions of all are pooled for the common good.

62. National-local relationships. National and local community relations agencies play complementary roles in the general community relations program.

How General Are the General Principles?

The foregoing statements of principles have been presented as general guidelines for Jewish community relations in the United States today. How, then, can their values and their limitations be assessed?

Three questions can be considered regarding the general applicability of these principles:

1. How generally can they be applied to Jewish community relations activities in this country?
2. How generally can they be applied to problems of intergroup relations in the United States, not those specifically involving the Jewish community?
3. How generally can they be applied to problems of Jewish community relations in countries other than the United States?

Jewish Community Relations Activities in the United States

Many observations have been made about the specific application of the various principles to real-life questions. A summary statement is that general principles are aids in approaching the specific questions of action, not determinants.

There is an inherent ambiguity in applying general statements to specific situations. With sixty-two statements, and an infinite variation in events as they occur, only approximate matches can be expected. Take principle Number 24, for instance: How is "merit" to be assessed in real life? Or Number 32: Is a particular utterance defamatory prejudice, or is it a harsh but fair judgment, within the bounds of democratic give-and-take? Or Number 15: How does a "cult" differ from your religion and my religion?

The general statements are intended to be reasonably consistent with each other at the level of principle, but it is not always a simple matter to decide how to apply them simultaneously in practice. For instance, might not Number 13, upholding civil liberties, clash with measures of exposure or quarantine or police action taken under Number 14 to protect against anti-Semitic acts or threats? Or, when is an action helpful in dispelling misinformation, as in principle Number 33, and not simply an exhortation of goodwill, which is designated in Number 41 as ineffectual?

These are just a few examples to demonstrate that fresh analysis and planning are always essential. But with the help of general principles it should not be necessary to go back to Square One every time. Each principle suggests a consideration that should be weighed in current deliberations. When it seems to be applicable, a whole course of possible actions to be considered, and a number of mistakes to be avoided, become available without the need to reinvent every detail. If the principle is deemed inapplicable to the instant situation, it will at least have stimulated some focused discussion and a sharper analysis.

For instance, let us suppose that an anti-Israel editorial appears in an influential local paper one morning. The responsible leaders of the Jewish community might consider Number 45, about combating negative images; Numbers 42 and 43, about targeting communications; Number 48, about interpretation of Israel. They might reflect, in accordance with Numbers 8, 36, and 46, about whether they have built up a sufficient reservoir of favorable contacts in their community to call upon in time of need. This presupposes that they have previously applied Numbers 57 and 61, and have already developed an effective process for cooperating systematically and dealing in a coordinated way with whatever challenge comes along.

Of course other principles are also relevant. Each is stated separately for clarity, but they should all be regarded as an interrelated set. And of course no leader or professional has to thumb a book of principles every day. Knowledgeable and experienced people think more or less along these lines without prompting.

Thus while the principles do not constitute an infallible compendium of answers to all questions, they can be helpful in meeting actual, and not just hypothetical, situations.

Intergroup Relations Generally in the United States

These principles have been written in terms of the community relations processes of the American Jewish community. They are drawn from the experience and the deliberations of Jewish agencies and organizations. They certainly do not apply without adaptation to other aspects of community interrelationships in our country today.

On the other hand, as has just been discussed in the preceding section, even for Jews there is no automatic application of general principles to arrive at sure-fire specific answers. A number of the statements could probably be helpful, with analysis, even to groups whose situation, history, and requirements are quite different from those of the American Jewish community.

The blacks, involuntary migrants to this country as slaves, have had a history of brutal repression and deprivation, quite different from the Jewish experience in the United States. They also have a long and honorable experience in attempting to cope with their own community relations problems. The Hispanics are just beginning to coalesce into a self-recognizing group; Mexicans and Puerto Ricans and Cubans differ widely among themselves. Groups descended from Polish and from Irish immigrants are involved in active programs of interpretation today. Many other groups have distinctive needs.

129 / How General are the General Principles

Is there anything that matches these diverse experiences with particular principles of Jewish community relations?

The policy statements (Numbers 1 through 8) are probably applicable to all groups in the United States. For reasons of semantics, not substance, Number 3, the principle that no group in this country should be considered "majority" or "minority," may seem unattractive to official "minority" groups, but this same policy worded differently would probably be well accepted. Policy Number 5, the American Creed, may evoke cynicism from the blacks and Hispanics and Native Americans and other groups that may feel they have seen little evidence of the presumed ideal of equality. They should remember, however, that it was in connection with the "American dilemma" of unequal treatment of blacks that Gunnar Myrdal articulated the idea of the American Creed so forcefully. As a policy, rather than an actuality, this principle can perhaps be helpful to blacks and Hispanics and other disadvantaged groups.

Some of the principles that deal with Jewish security (Numbers 9 through 17) may be too specific to translate in terms of other situations, and those regarding religious freedom (Numbers 26 through 29) may be of interest chiefly to small religious bodies. The leadership of various groups may find it useful to consider Numbers 13, 14, and 16, and Numbers 30 through 36.

On the other hand, the sections on social and economic justice (Numbers 18 through 25), the public schools (Numbers 37 through 40), and the mass media of communication (Numbers 41 through 46) may be relevant to the concerns of all groups. Principle Number 24, regarding merit, is not in itself counter to current black strategy, but there is a major semantic difference: "quota" to blacks means a foothold in the job market; to Jews it means an exclusionary *numerus clausus,* the negation of merit.

While the section regarding world Jewry (Numbers 47 through 55) may seem to be very specific, the concern of blacks for the African nations and of a great variety of ethnic groups for their countries of family origin may supply parallels that would warrant consideration by their leadership.

Finally, the guidelines for Jewish community organization embodied in the procedural principles (Numbers 56 through 62) are completely specific. Even so, there have been somewhat parallel developments within other groups.

Unfortunately, the widest divergence of applicability occurs with regard to a group that heavily overlaps the Jewish (and every other self-recognizing) group—women. The subordination of women has had a different origin from most forms of intergroup conflict, and tension reflects different motivation and different social forces. Some of the strategic principles of intergroup relationships and the use of the media may apply to the struggle for women's rights, but beyond that there is probably little that is applicable. Even the policy statements, except for Numbers 1 and 8 (the general welfare, and coalition), may not apply to the very special problems of male-female relationships.

There are other groups to whom the principles may be useful, namely, public officials, academics, and other people in a position to advance good intergroup relations, but who are not functioning as leaders of any of the self-recognizing groups. Perhaps they can find applications of the principles that can help in understanding or easing certain difficult situations. If that proves possible, all to the good.

Jewish Community Relations Outside the United States

How general are the principles in their application to Jewish communities in other countries? The policies and principles are quite specific to the American scene. Even in Canada, perhaps the nearest match to the United States, whole sections would be inapplicable—regarding church-state relationships, for instance—because of differences in Canada's basic laws.

On the other hand, problems regarding Jewish security may be similar in a number of countries. Characteristics of the media may also be reasonably similar, as may be relationships with Jews in other countries (this applies, of course, to Jewish communities in free democratic settings). Jewish community organization may have some similarities, but even technical differences—such as questions of tax laws—as well as the size and composition of the Jewish community and its traditional place in the general society can make large differences.

It is plainly a risky business to try to transpose the principles to another setting. If they stimulate leaders of Jewish groups abroad to examine their own principles, that itself could be of value.

Notes and References

1. Cf. "The NJCRAC—What It Is and How It Works" (hereafter cited as NJ), p. 4 [Samuel Spiegler].
2. Cf. "Joint Program Plan 1981–82" (hereafter cited as JPP 81–82), p. 3.
3. Cf. JPP 81–82, p. 3.
4. Cf. "NJCRAC—Statement of Purpose" (hereafter cited as Purp), p. ii. See also NJ, p. 2.
5. Cf. "Statement of Qualifications," Association of Jewish Community Relations Workers, 1956.
6. JPP 81–82, p. 3.
7. See JPP 81–82, p. 3.
8. Ibid., pp. 26–27 et passim.
9. Cf. Report of NJCRAC Reassessment Conference of Community Relations Work with Children and Youth, 1957 (hereafter cited as C&Y), pp. 26–27; see also JPP 81–82, p. 3.
10. Cf. C&Y, pp. 26–27.
11. Cf. ibid.
12. See Robert M. MacIver, "Report on the Jewish Community Relations Agencies," 1951, p. 36.
13. See *Jewish Public Affairs: A Source Book,* San Francisco JCRC, 1975 (hereafter cited as JPA), pp. 9–10. [Earl Raab.]
14. See Benjamin R. Epstein in "Programming Jewish Community Relations in the Present Period" (hereafter cited as Prog.), 1947, p. 22. See also Gunnar Myrdal, *An American Dilemma* (20th Anniversary Edition, Harper and Row, 1964), passim.
15. Cf. David Petegorsky in Prog., p. 34.
16. Cf. "How to Organize for Jewish Community Relations" (hereafter cited as How), NCRAC, 1955, p. 12. [Jules Cohen.]
17. Cf. ibid.
18. See specific citations in these references.
19. Cf. JPP 81–82, p. 29.
20. See "Combating Anti-Semitism Today," report of an NJCRAC Reassessment Conference, 1968 (hereafter cited as A-S), p. 9.
21. JPP 81–82, p. 27.
22. Cf. A-S, p. 13.
23. Cf. JPP 81–82, p. 29.
24. See A-S, p. 13.
25. Cf. A-S, p. 8; see also pp. 13–15.
26. Cf. NCRAC Reassessment Conference Report of "The Uses of Law for the Advancement of Community Relations," 1955 (hereafter cited as Law), p. 57.

27. JPP 81–82, p. 30.
28. Cf. A-S, p. 17. See also Report of NCRAC Reassessment Conference, "Overt Forms of Anti-Semitism," 1953 (hereafter cited as Overt), pp. 50–51, and A-S, p. 16.
29. Cf. JPP 81–82, p. 39.
30. Cf. A-S, p. 17. See also Overt, p. 48 and p. 53.
31. Cf. A-S, p. 19.
32. Cf. Petegorsky in Prog, pp. 33–36.
33. Cf. JPP 81–82, p. 21. See also JPA, pp. 119–121.
34. Cf. Law, p. 57.
35. Cf. Report of NCRAC Reassessment Conference, "Respective Roles and Responsibilities of Private and Public Agencies in the Advancement of Community Relations Objectives," 1958 (hereafter cited as P&P), p. 28.
36. See JPP 71–72, pp. 16–17.
37. See JPP 81–82, passim.
38. Cf. JPP 77–78, p. 32.
39. JPP 81–82, p. 26.
40. Ibid.
41. Cf. ibid.
42. Cf. Law, p. 58. See also John Slawson, Benjamin Epstein, and David Petegorsky, in Prog, passim.
43. Cf. "Safeguarding Religious Liberty," Joint Advisory Committee of the Synagogue Council of America and the NJCRAC, 1971 (hereafter cited as Safe), p. 5.
44. Cf. ibid. See also Safe, pp. 6–11.
45. Cf. Safe, p. 3. See also Report of NCRAC Reassessment Conference on "Religion and the Public School," 1959, (hereafter cited as R&S), pp. 46–56.
46. Cf. Safe, p. 12. See also R&S, p. 40.
47. Cf. C&Y, p. 26.
48. Cf. Report of NCRAC Reassessment Conference, "Community Relations Values of Interreligious Activities," 1953 (hereafter cited as Int), p. 28. See also C&Y, p. 28; R&S, p. 44.
49. Cf. C&Y, p. 28. See also Int, pp. 34–35.
50. Cf. C&Y, p. 28. See also Int, pp. 36–37, and Report of NCRAC Reassessment Conference, "The Use of the Mass Media of Communication for Community Relations Purposes," 1956 (hereafter cited as MM), p. 23.
51. Cf. C&Y, p. 27. See also Int, p. 33.
52. Willis Hawley, Dean of Peabody College, chaired a commission sponsored by the Center for Educational and Human Development Policy, Institute for Policy Studies of Vanderbilt University, which issued a multivolume series of studies under the general title "Assessment of Current Knowledge about the Effects of School Desegregation Strategie." The first volume was published in April of 1981.
53. Cf. Law, p. 47. See also Law, pp. 49–50.
54. Cf. C&Y, p. 27, and Int, p. 37.
55. Cf. Report of NJCRAC Reassessment Conference, "The Public Schools and American Democratic Pluralism—The Role of the Jewish Community," 1971 (hereafter cited as Plu), pp. 22–24.
56. Cf. Plu, p. 21. See also Plu., pp. 26–27; C&Y, p. 32.

57. Cf. C&Y, p. 28, See also C&Y, pp. 29–30; Plu, pp. 22–24.
58. Cf. Plu, p. 25.
59. See MM, pp. 18–21.
60. Cf. MM, pp. 23–24.
61. Cf. MM, p. 25.
62. Cf. Report of NJCRAC Reassessment Conference, "The Mass Media, The Image of Israel, and U.S. Foreign Policy," 1980 (hereafter cited as Isr), p. 18. See also Isr, p. 22.
63. Cf. Isr, p. 18. See also Isr, pp. 19–22; MM. p. 27.
64. Cf. Isr, p. 23, See also MM, pp. 28–29.
65. See S. A. Fineberg, "The Strategy of Error," *Contemporary Jewish Record*, 1945.
66. Cf. Isr, p. 23.
67. Cf. JPP 81–82, p. 16.
68. Cf. Isr, p. 20. See also Isr, p. 5; Isr, pp. 19–21; "Fostering Understanding of the Situation in the Middle East," NJCRAC, 1977 (hereafter cited as Fos), p. 3, pp. 6–7, pp. 13–14; JPP 81–82, pp. 7–8.
69. Cf. Fos, p. 4.
70. JPP 81–82, p. 9.
71. See JPP 77–78, p. 11.
72. Cf. JPP 81–82, pp. 13–15.
73. Cf. JPP 81–82, pp. 15–16.
74. Cf. JPP 81–82, p. 27.
75. Cf. JPP 81–82, pp. 17–18.
76. Cf. JPP 81–82, p. 19.
77. Cf. NJ, p. 2.
78. Cf. How, p. 9. See also Report of NJCRAC Reassessment Conference, "Community Relations Components in the Work of Other Jewish Communal Services," 1961 (hereafter cited as CRC), p. 25.
79. Cf. Purp, p. i.
80. Cf. CRC, p. 28. See also CRC, pp. 36–38.
81. Cf. How, p. 9.
82. Adapted from Purp, pp. i–iii, and NJ, pp. 2–5.
83. Purp, pp. iii–iv.

For further reading:

Berger, Graenum (ed.): *The Turbulent Decades: Jewish Communal Services in America 1958–1978* (2 vols.). Conference of Jewish Communal Service, New York, 1981. See especially articles by John Slawson, Arnold Aronson, Isaac Franck, Earl Raab, and Albert D. Chernin, pp. 537–608, Vol. I; by Philip Bernstein, Charles Miller, Arthur Hertzberg, Solomon Geld, Irving Greenberg, Morris Grumer, Albert D. Chernin, Walter J. Ackerman, Walter A. Lurie, Harold Arian, and Sidney Z. Vincent, pp. 821–924, Vol. II; and by Martha K. Selig, Jacob H. Kravitz, Philip Jacobson, and Karl D. Zukerman, pp. 1271–1317, Vol. II.

Freeman, Julian: *Organizing the American Jewish Community.* Council of Jewish Federations, New York, 1977.

Lurie, Harry L.: *A Heritage Affirmed.* Jewish Publication Society of America, Philadelphia, 1961.

Lurie, Walter A.: "Intergroup Relations." In Volume I (pp. 668–676) *Encyclopedia of School Work,* Seventeenth Issue, National Association of Social Workers, New York, 1971.

Lurie, Walter A. "Yes and No—Living with Ambivalence: Intergroup Relations in the United States Today." *Jewish Social Work Forum,* Vol. 8, 1, Spring 1971, pp. 5–24.

Lurie, Walter A.: "Thirty Years of Professional Development in Jewish Community Relations." [Commissioned by the Association of Jewish Community Relations Workers, 1980.] *Journal of Jewish Communal Service,* 1982, Vol. 58.

Minkoff, Isaiah M.: "Development of Jewish Communal Organization in America 1900–1956." In *Two Generations in Perspective: Notable Events and Trends 1896–1956,* edited by Harry Schneiderman, pp. 110–138. Monde Publishers, New York, 1957.

Wolfe, Ann G.: *A Reader in Jewish Community Relations.* KTAV Publishing House, for Association of Jewish Community Relations Workers, New York, 1975.

Index

THE AUTHOR

Walter A. Lurie is a social psychologist (Ph.D., University of Chicago, 1935). He served as Program Analyst from 1946 until 1956, and as Director of Program Reassessment from 1968 until 1980, of the National Jewish Community Relations Advisory Council. He is the author of the articles on "Intergroup Relations" in the *Encyclopedia of Social Work* (1971) and its two predecessor Year Books, as well as of many contributions to professional journals. He has been Director of the Large City Budgeting Conference (Council of Jewish Federations) and of the Jewish Vocational Service of Chicago, and is a past president of the Conference of Jewish Communal Service and of the Association of Jewish Community Relations Workers. Dr. Lurie is a Fellow of the American Psychological Association and a Charter Member of the Society for the Psychological Study of Social Issues.